Needle Lace Flowers

Figen Cakir

Search Press

A Quantum Book

Published in 2013 by Search Press Ltd.
Wellwood, North Farm Road,
Tunbridge Wells,
Kent TN2 3DR

This book is produced by
Quantum Publishing
6 Blundell Street
London
N7 9BH

ISBN 978-1-78221-005-4

QUMNLFW

Publisher: Sarah Bloxham
Managing Editor: Samantha Warrington
Editor: Anna Southgate
Assistant Editor: Jo Morley
Consultant Editor: Caroline Smith
Designer: Louise Turpin
Illustrators: Stephen Dew and Tim Scrivens
Photographer: Simon Pask
Production Manager: Rohana Yusof

Printed in China by Hung Hing Printing (China) Co., Ltd

Contents

Oya Needle Lace

The moment I first laid eyes on oya needlework was not as profound as one might imagine. With the maternal side of my family living in Istanbul, I would visit Turkey almost every summer as a child, and the experience was always an intense riot of colour, sound and smell. It was customary for flower-sellers and local shopkeepers to have colourful scarves wound around their heads, the trims of which looked unique, but so perfect and so brightly coloured that you would be forgiven for thinking they were artificially made or a part of the fabric.

Being a girl, I was gifted many oya-trimmed garments of my own. With each visit over the years, I managed to garner quite a collection of beautiful headscarves and linen, each with its own memory of when it had been given and by whom. It was only natural for me to be given these gifts – handmade items for the home are a major part of the traditional Turkish trousseau. Starting when a girl is born, chests full of handcrafted linens and clothing are created over many years and then stored, layered with lavender bags, sprigs of dried thyme and pure rose-essence soap to keep them fresh and clean smelling, until that girl's wedding day. The tradition continues to this day, regardless of wealth, education or location. Nowadays, however, many mothers employ other craftswomen to make a trousseau for their daughters, or they buy ready-made items from special trousseau shops, either because they have not learned the handicrafts themselves or they simply do not have the time.

AGE-OLD TRADITION
Turkey is a unique place. A country so unexpectedly modern in many aspects, it follows trends along with the rest of the world, and yet it remains deeply loyal to age-old traditions when it comes to marriage. In classic Turkish tradition, still adhered to in many rural areas, daughters are not given away lightly and the groom may sometimes have to ask for her hand several times before he is deemed suitable.

Sometimes, in very rural and old-fashioned villages, a dowry may be requested. It is not unheard of for couples to elope if the potential groom cannot meet the demands made on him and the pair is unwilling to wait for him to save money. In Turkish tradition, while the groom's family meet the wedding costs, it is up to the bride's family to prepare and present a trousseau worthy of their precious daughter. The contents of this trousseau are then proudly displayed about the bridal home for all to come and view the day before the wedding. And it is from this trousseau that thousands of years' worth of inherited craft and talent spills forth. Every colour imaginable is used to trim scarves, guest towels and household linen with oya needle lace and classic crochet.

SO WHAT IS OYA?
Oya, or *igne oyasi* (pronounced eeneh o-yahsi) as it is also commonly known, is an intricate form of crochet made using silky thread and a small sewing or darning needle to create a series of tiny loops and knots. It is a needlecraft that requires patience and careful attention – so much so that it has earned a place among Turkish idioms that relate to things

RIGHT: Pieces from a bride's trousseau might include practical wares for the home, such as table linen, but also decorative pieces to wear. Traditionally, pieces are trimmed by hand, using oya needle lace techniques.

that require painstaking effort. For example, *oya gibi* means 'difficult like oya' and the verb *oyalamak*, 'to put off or delay', is used to mean an act that keeps lengthening in time. Once you start to make flowers of your own, you will see that these idioms have arisen with good reason.

Although the techniques used to make oya needle lace are relatively simple and repetitive, it can take time to progress to the more adventurous designs, so it is worth bearing in mind that it is a slow and time-consuming art. Nevertheless, it is one that will give endless pleasure, because you will be improving your skill with practice at the same time as mastering the first type of crochet ever known.

BELOW: An Anatolian lace-maker trims a bright-coloured scarf. She is crocheting oya flowers to match the flower motifs in the fabric.

My Oya

For me, what started as a passing interest in oya needle lace developed into a deep-rooted passion over time. Having received little gifts here and there, I began to do research into the background of oya. At first it seemed daunting to try making oya needle lace for myself, and I satisfied my interest in the craft by reading about it, seeking it out and watching seasoned crafters at work.

This only made the craft appear more difficult and I was convinced I would be incapable of mastering such a fine art (sometimes referred to as the most difficult needlecraft in the world). Finally, a couple of years ago, I decided to overcome my fear of failure and try it for myself – I wanted to feel the thread twist and knot in my fingers, and to experience in practice what I had already discovered over a decade's research.

During the first few months, I struggled to reconcile my extensive knowledge of oya with my seeming inability to create it. My instructors – local Turkish housewives in my neighbourhood, whose fingers could hold and shape a mass of threads with alarming dexterity – assured me that it had taken them years to perfect every aspect of oya needle lace, having been introduced to the craft aged ten or thereabouts. Although that assurance did not serve to make me feel any better, as they had obviously had a head start of about three decades on me, I was determined not to fail them in their tutelage.

I now love to make leaves and flowers of all kinds and do so with considerable skill. Many of my pieces mimic their counterparts in the natural world, while others have no equivalent in nature. In making this book, I have had the pleasure of working with women from my local Turkish community and of combining the extensive knowledge of these naturally talented women with my own designs and vision. I am grateful to destiny, for bringing me to this small, modern Turkish town just a couple of hours outside of Istanbul, where I am lucky to meet someone new and talented every day.

ABOVE: This village woman wears a headscarf that she has trimmed with three rows of intricate oya lacework.

Oya History

Traditional Turkish arts and decorative crafts are very distinctive in their appearance, colour and style. They immediately stand out in any setting or medium. The role of oya needle lace in this is as a complementary craft; it adds a touch of completion wherever it is applied.

It is not known for certain where oya first originated, although research points to Anatolia. Oya needle lace was certainly known to traders travelling along the Silk Route connecting eastern, southern and western Asia with the Mediterranean and Europe, and the first Europeans to be introduced to it were the French, around the 13th century. At the time, many crafts

RIGHT: The sultans of the Ottoman Empire were great patrons of the decorative arts and many crafts flourished during this time, including painting, carpet-weaving, book-binding and calligraphy.

BELOW: Many of the handcrafts that developed in Europe from the Middle Ages onwards were influenced by examples coming from the East, with knitting, crochet and embroidery among them.

LEFT: These embroidered black and green Turkish scarves have been trimmed with colourful shapes and flowers.

East and Asia. It may be called *oyu* or *oyuma* in different dialects. Despite losing popularity during the post-war Republic era of the 1920s – and even more so in more recent years – oya has nonetheless managed to survive, thanks to the long-standing tradition of making gifts for young brides. In addition to this, the craft has always been an important pastime for women in rural areas, especially Anatolia.

BASIC OYA MATERIALS

Silk was the primary material used for making textiles during the Ottoman era, used in everything from rug-making to clothing and tents. The Turks have a history of silk farming that dates from around the 16th century, and before this it was produced in Iran. It was, for several centuries, extremely popular and a major commercial product for traders from other countries. As well as silk, cotton was a popular choice for making textiles, especially as cotton farming was, and remains, such a big part of Turkish agriculture. Even today it is ranked as the most luxurious quality cotton in the world.

Nowadays silk can now be expensive and difficult to find. From around the 1960s women began to use cotton, nylon and polyester blend threads. As well as being more easily available and economical, these withstand modern cleaning methods and detergents a great deal better than silk would.

While oya uses thread predominantly, beads are also added in some regions. Beads have always played a big role in Turkish traditions – the evil eye amulet made of glass is of Turkish origin – and were used to adorn tents and horses. Turkish women traditionally dressed in magnificent colour and splendour, with much jewellery.

OYA LACE-MAKING TRADITIONS

Oya needle lace is a craft that is carried out in almost every region of Turkey, the techniques and materials changing from region to region depending on culture and tradition. Some varieties are created using fine

and innovations were brought back to the West by merchants and many countries, among them Spain and Italy, were greatly influenced by the weaving and knitting techniques of the East, taking inspiration from colourful patterned socks and garments made between the 12th and 16th centuries.

IMPERIAL HERITAGE

Oya, as a word, means 'to embellish, to craft something that takes time' and in the 2nd century, Turks also used the term to mean, 'the house is embellished'. During the Ottoman Empire era (c.1300–1900), great importance was placed upon interior and exterior decoration and the arts were given enormous appreciation. The Ottomans were very artistically inclined and this is evident in their architecture, textiles, works of art and literature. Decorative crafts from all over the empire were brought together and traditional weaving and oya from Anatolia were both greatly valued, especially in the imperial palace. Having been practised widely throughout the Ottoman Empire, evidence of the craft can still be seen in many countries besides Turkey, including those of the Balkans, the Middle

crochet hooks, round bone or wood shuttles or U-shaped metal lengths identical to hairpins.

Out of all the traditional needlecrafts, oya is probably the most 'vocal'. Its motifs send very clear and specific messages, and their purpose is to communicate feelings and events (see The Language of Oya). As a result oya motifs have been given very unique names, sometimes sad and sometimes amusing, over the centuries. Because oya is so beautiful and intricate, the phrase 'like oya' has, over time, come refer to something beautiful or well crafted.

While the same designs may come out of different regions, the meanings of specific motifs can differ widely. However, the emotions they convey remain the same: happiness, love, rejection, death, hate, desire, hopes and wishes are all represented. A particular style, symbol, colour or flower is used to convey an emotion, or event in one's life. While

there are many crafts all over the world that have been used since the beginning of time to convey a message, there is none more personal or lively as oya, or any that have survived so completely with their individual meanings.

THE LANGUAGE OF OYA

There is great symbolism to be found in the motifs of oya needle lace, many of which represent themes of life: birth, marriage and death. Such symbolism comes from folk culture, where motifs once played an important role in society, primarily functioning as

BELOW: Despite the tremendous amount of work that goes into trimming garments with oya needlework lace, many of the pieces are worn as everyday items of clothing.

a means of communication between the women in a community, who were otherwise expected to keep their thoughts to themselves. Over many hundreds of years, the same motifs have inevitably inspired folk songs and love poems.

This symbolism consists of both simple and complicated motifs made up of symbols, digits, letters, living or decorative objects. Each one carries a strong power of thought and the various meanings have not come about by coincidence – each one and its uses are pre-meditated and planned.

The most common tales woven into the fine, silky threads of oya needle lace were those alluding to the relationships between husband and wife or new bride and mother-in-law. This is not surprising since people in all cultures have at one time been part of a large family with the in-laws at the helm. Motifs such as grass mean peace and happiness, for example; gravestones mean faith and mortality; caterpillars represent enemies. They were all used to convey intense and deep messages. Traditionally,

a bride who was greatly unhappy or angry with her mother-in-law might wear a headscarf trimmed with gravestone motifs and the message would be that she wanted her out of her world and that she would keep her grudge until both their dying days. A woman who was unhappy with her lot in life, or whose husband had left her would cry her woes into needle lace motifs of passion flowers.

While no specific date or person in history is credited with the names given to oya designs, it appears that they were passed down by word of mouth among women and spread in that way. Many examples of the folk language of oya are apparent in the colloquial names that exist for the motifs, and are often very tongue-in-cheek: 'mother-in-law tongue', 'the barber's mirror', 'laughing baby', 'eyelash oya' are some examples of this. The most popular is the

BELOW: This sampler from Cyprus dates to the early 20th century and shows similar motifs to those in oya needle lace. They, too, are imbued with symbolism.

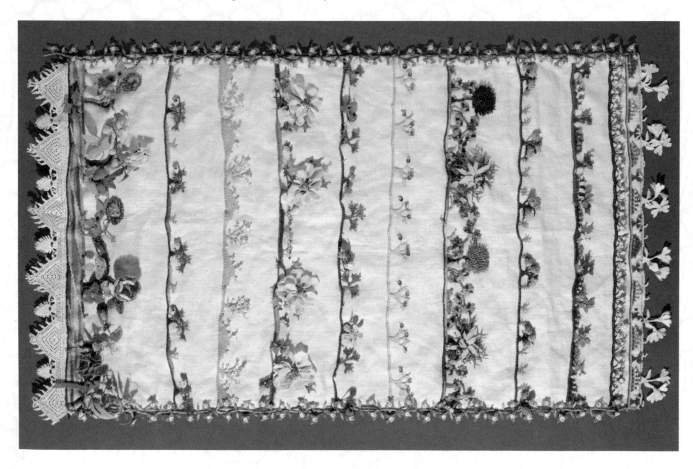

red chilli pepper oya, commonly used – in the past – by brides who did not get on well with their mothers-in-law and expressed this by saying 'our relationship is as bitter and hot as the chilli pepper'.

When beginning my research into oya needle lace several years ago, I was left in awe of the sheer audacity expressed through such motifs. It can not have been easy for women in past centuries, and it seems to me a sign of strength and courage to display symbols so publicly, where the meanings were so distinctive and the messages so clear. It seems that women had no intention of keeping silent or showing meekness – that is, if the names given to the oya needle lace motifs are anything to go by.

NOT JUST FOR GIRLS

Although oya is viewed as a predominantly female decoration, it often featured in menswear as well. In such instances oya motifs included secret or silent messages sent from young girls who were forbidden from speaking to men. Many a time, oya was used as a secret letter – either a declaration of love or an admonishment to a suitor who has his eye elsewhere. A village lad, for example, might wear a fringe of oya on a wrapped, turban-style, headscarf made by a young girl waiting to be wed. Men would also have oya-trimmed pouches to hold their money. Traditionally the handkerchiefs and the undershirts of a groom would also be trimmed with oya.

Today, oya needle lace is appreciated simply for being a very intricate and beautiful craft. It is worthwhile, however, to spare a thought for some of their meanings in the past and to remember the rich stories associated with them!

RIGHT: A watercolour of a Turkish Tartar, or government messenger, dated c. 1845–1855. You can see that his clothes are elaborately trimmed with tassels and embroidery.

Using this Book

Needle Lace Flowers presents 16 flower projects based on seasonal blooms.
Each project features easy-to-follow steps with schematic diagrams.
The techniques that are used to make the flowers are collected in a reference
chapter towards the end of the book. That way, they are always easily found.
Again, each technique is demonstrated using simple illustrations.

Before starting anything, make sure you have your tools and materials to hand. This will not be difficult, as there are very few needed. The projects simply require threads in your chosen colours, a darning or sewing needle and a small pair of sharp scissors (see box opposite).

Although the steps you will be following to make the flowers are straightforward and repetitive, it will take some practice to perfect the technique. A good way to begin is to work through the basic techniques (see pages 106–126) a few times so that you become used to handling the thread. It won't matter what shapes you make at this stage – simply get used to making basic loops using the various methods, and to add new thread so that your work remains seamless. Once you have perfected a very tight knot and fairly good-shaped loops, you will be ready to try your hand at one of the simpler patterns.

Once you do make a start on the flower projects, do not be too distressed if your flowers turn out a little different each time, or do not resemble the ones in this book. Think of flowers in nature, and how they are all differently shaped and unique, even those of the same variety. And think of the women all those centuries ago who created their own language with oya shapes, mimicking what it was they saw in their surroundings – they all adapted the colours and shapes to their own whims to convey messages of unspoken words.

Each flower project comes with a rough guide as to how long it takes to make. This is a guideline only, and then for those who have mastered the craft. Because the work is tiring on the eyes and fingers, it is advisable to spend a maximum of only two to three hours in a day on a flower so expect it to take anything from three days to a week when making any one of the flower projects in the book from start to finish, including its showcase project.

OYA TIPS

• Work slowly! The best results always arise from adopting a slow, methodical approach.

• Practise with brightly coloured thread at first. This will help you to see your shapes more clearly and make it more fun.

• If you are not used to working with sharp sewing needles, you can practise with a blunt darning needle. This is a particularly good idea when learning how to hold the thread and make the knots, so that you avoid pricking yourself by mistake. Once you have mastered the craft, you can progress to something shorter and sharper.

• If, during a flower project, you need to stop and take up the work at a later date, make an enlarged copy of the schematic illustration and write notes on it so that you know where to start up next time.

You will need

- **Thread:** Projects tend to be worked using one continuous thread, so 25m/80ft balls or skeins are recommended. The type of thread you choose is up to you – we recommend DMC Perlé #5 or Lizbeth size 20, both widely available in a wide range of colours.
- **Needle:** A short, sharp sewing needle is best, as this will allow you to make your knots extremely tight and firm. This will, in turn, help you to make flowers with neater, smaller loops. Thicker, blunter needles tend to make knots that come loose.
- **Scissors:** A good-quality, sharp-pointed pair of scissors.

SCHEMATIC KEY

The schematic diagrams for the flower projects use the following key. For the sake of clarity, base loops do not appear in a schematic diagram, unless they form a Row or Round of a stem, leaf or petal.

∩	Open loop to show the first Round 1 of a stem		Picot
○	Closed loop used for making each row		Double picot
●	Seed knot		Triple picot
		⌒	Long loop between picots

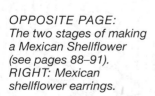

OPPOSITE PAGE:
The two stages of making a Mexican Shellflower (see pages 88–91).
RIGHT: Mexican shellflower earrings.

Flower Gallery

With inspiration taken from popular garden plants and wildflowers, the 16 blooms for this book have been chosen for their diversity in colour and petal shape. Arranged by season, they offer great scope for making a wide range of projects of your own design.

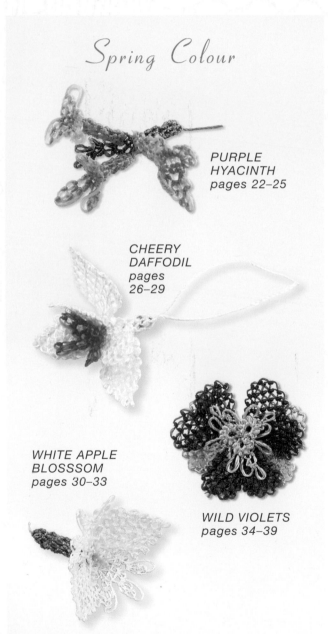

Spring Colour

PURPLE HYACINTH
pages 22–25

CHEERY DAFFODIL
pages 26–29

WHITE APPLE BLOSSSOM
pages 30–33

WILD VIOLETS
pages 34–39

Summer Charm

WHITE JASMINE
pages 42–45

PRETTY FORGET-ME-NOTS
pages 46–49

DAINTY DAISY
pages 56–59

ORIENTAL LILY
pages 50–55

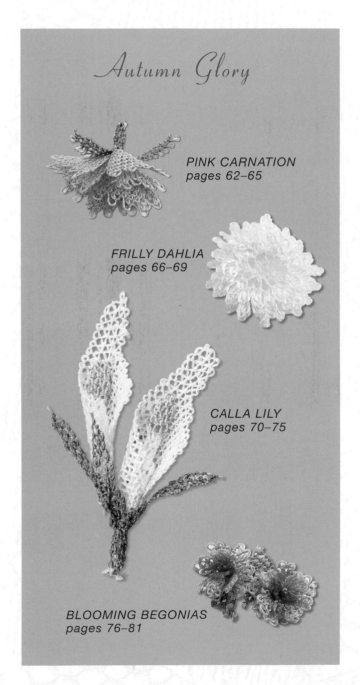

Autumn Glory

PINK CARNATION
pages 62–65

FRILLY DAHLIA
pages 66–69

CALLA LILY
pages 70–75

BLOOMING BEGONIAS
pages 76–81

Winter Cheer

MEXICAN SHELLFLOWER
pages 88–91

WINTER ROSE
pages 84–87

FESTIVE POINSETTIA
pages 92–97

ELEGANT CHRYSANTHEMUM
pages 98–103

Spring Colour

Purple hyacinths, cheery daffodils, white apple blossom
and wild violets provide the perfect inspiration for the
projects in this chapter. Their delicate petal shapes
and bright spring colours are characteristic of many
flowers that appear at this time of year.

Purple Hyacinth

These are probably some of the jolliest oya flowers to make, because of the way in which they sway prettily as you move if you are wearing them as jewellery. In oya language, hyacinths have different meanings depending on their colours. White hyacinths represent loyalty and commitment; blue-purple hyacinths announce that the girl wearing them is in love – worn as trim on a pink scarf; pink hyacinths declare that the girl is engaged to be married. More generally, hyacinths are used to symbolise hope, love and chastity.

You will need

- 1 x 25m (80ft) skein green thread
- 1 x 25m (80ft) skein lilac thread
- Sewing needle
- Scissors

Skill level 🌸

Time 5 hours

Inspiration

Hyacinthus orientalis grows widely in the temperate world and has early-flowering, strongly fragrant flowers.

Stem, leaf and flower head are made as one single unit.

STEM AND LEAF

1 Start by making the stem. Cast on using green thread (see pages 106–107) and make a three-loop base (see pages 108–109).

2 Working from right to left, make three loops to form Round 1 of the stem. Fold in half and secure with a knot (see pages 110–111).

3 Working in the round, make a further three rounds of three loops followed by four rounds of four loops (see pages 112–113). Make the additional loop on Round 5 in any loop below (see page 116). Make the loops on Round 8 slightly larger. Do not cast off.

4 With the stem complete, now make the leaf (see pages 114–115). Working from left to right, make two loops in any loop on Round 8 of the stem. This will form Row 1 of the leaf.

5 Your thread should be to the right of your work. Make a reverse knot and work another two loops. Continue to work in this way, until you have four rows of two loops. Cast off tightly and cut the thread close to the knot (see page 126).

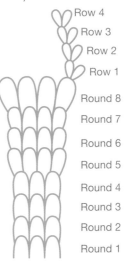

Row 4
Row 3
Row 2
Row 1
Round 8
Round 7
Round 6
Round 5
Round 4
Round 3
Round 2
Round 1

Actual Size

FLOWER HEAD

1 Using lilac thread, cast on in any remaining loop on Round 8 of the stem (see pages 122–123). Make three loops to form Round 1 of the flower. Then fold in half and secure with a knot.

2 Working in the round, make a further seven rounds of three loops, making sure that the loops on Round 8 are slightly larger than on the previous rounds.

3 For Round 9, make a double picot in each loop on Round 8 (see pages 119–121). Cast off when the third double picot is complete.

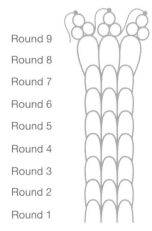

Round 9
Round 8
Round 7
Round 6
Round 5
Round 4
Round 3
Round 2
Round 1

4 Repeat Steps 1–3 to make another flower in each of the two remaining loops on Round 8 of the stem.

Hyacinth Keyring

These little hyacinths are perfect for dangly objects, as they bob and sway merrily with movement. They would feature nicely as part of a piece of jewellery – a pendant necklace, a charm on a bracelet, or even as a pair of earrings. Or you could use them to liven up items in the home – as a pretty decoration on curtain ties in the kitchen or attached to the zip-pull of a make-up bag.

To attach to a keyring, as shown here, take a jewellery-making pin and thread it through a pretty bead, and then through the stem of the hyacinth. Using small pliers, bend the end of the pin around a trigger snap. Repeat with as many hyacinths as you like and then clip the trigger snap onto a jump ring, for your keys.

Cheery Daffodil

These bright, cheerful, springtime flowers have featured in oya for centuries as an expression of unrequited love. Women who made them to wear in their hair, or for trimming their waistcoats and headscarves, silently sent out the message that they were the subject of hopeless love. It is no coincidence that the daffodil is named after the ancient Greek mythological legend of Narcissus. He broke the hearts of many young women, but ultimately fell in love with his own reflection. His fate was to die of grief on finding his love unrequited.

You will need

- 1 x 25m (80ft) skein yellow thread
- 1 x 25m (80ft) skein orange thread
- Sewing needle
- Scissors

Skill level ❀ ❀

Time 3–4 hours

Inspiration

The many species of daffodil flower from early to late spring.

The flower is made of three separate units that are assembled at the end.

OUTER PETALS

1 Start by making the stem. Cast on using yellow thread (see pages 106–107) and make a three-loop base (see pages 108–109).

2 Working from right to left, make three loops to form Round 1 of the stem. Fold in half and secure with a knot (see pages 110–111).

3 Working in the round, make a further four rounds of three loops, making sure that the loops on Round 5 are slightly larger than on the previous rounds (see pages 112–113).

4 With the stem complete, now make the first petal. Working directly onto the stem, and from left to right, make three loops in any loop on Round 5 of the stem, to form Row 1 of the petal (see page 115).

5 Your thread should be to the right of your work. Make a reverse knot and continue to work as follows, increasing or decreasing at the end of each row (see pages 114–116):
Row 2: Four loops
Row 3: Five loops
Row 4: Four loops
Row 5: Three loops
Row 6: Two loops
Row 7: One loop

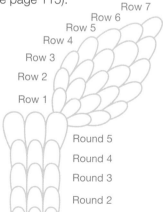

Row 7
Row 6
Row 5
Row 4
Row 3
Row 2
Row 1

Round 5
Round 4
Round 3
Round 2
Round 1

6 You have two options for continuing. The first is to cast off after the last knot on Row 7 of the petal (see page 126) and to cast on with new thread in the next large loop on Round 5 of the stem (see pages 122–123). Alternatively, if you have sufficient thread, you can work down one side of the petal in small loops to continue without casting off the thread. (see page 117).

7 Either way, follow Steps 4 to 6 to make a petal in each of the two remaining loops on Round 5 of the stem. Cast off after the last knot.

INNER PETALS

1 Cast on using yellow thread and make a three-loop base, leaving a tail of 10cm (4in). Working from right to left, make three loops for Round 1 of the stem. Fold in half and secure with a knot.

2 Working in the round, make a further four rounds of three loops, making sure that the loops on Round 5 are slightly larger than on the previous rounds.

3 With the stem complete, now make the first petal the same way as described for making the outer petals (see page 26), working the rows as follows:
Row 1: Two loops
Row 2: Three loops
Row 3: Four loops
Row 4: Three loops
Row 5: Two loops
Row 6: One loop

4 Continue as described for making the outer petals to make two more petals in the same way. Cast off after the last knot.

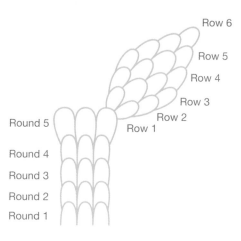

PICOT CENTRE

1 Start by making a small stem. Cast on using orange thread and, leaving a tail of 10cm (4in), make a two-loop base. Working from right to left, make two loops to form Round 1 of the stem. Fold the stem in half and secure with a knot.

2 Working in the round, continue as follows, making the additional loop on each round in any loop below (see page 116). Make the loops on Round 4 slightly larger than in the previous rounds:
Round 2: Three loops
Round 3: Four loops
Round 4: Five loops

3 For Round 5, make a double picot in each loop of Round 4 of the stem (see page 119–121). Cast off when the fifth double picot is complete.

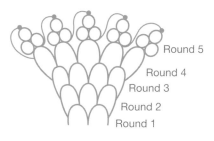

ASSEMBLY

Assemble the three units, following one of the two methods described (see pages 124–125). Make sure the inner and outer petals are not aligned with each other, but alternate with each other in the round. You may need to manipulate the pieces a little as you work to make sure that the inner stem sits snugly inside the outer. Make a few neat stitches here and there to secure the pieces together and cut any loose ends.

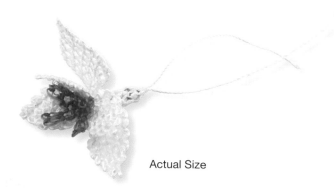

Actual Size

Daffodil Artwork

These bright, jolly daffodils make the perfect addition to a springtime celebration – a birthday or wedding, or Easter festivities. You can stitch them onto place mats and napkin rings, or use them with other spring flowers to make a floral centrepiece.

Have fun creating a quirky, three-dimensional artwork for a fancy frame. Find a piece of fabric larger than your frame. Use pins or tacking thread to mark the aperture of the frame on the fabric. Arrange the flowers within the space and stitch in place. Don't stitch too tightly – you want the daffodils to have slight movement. Fold the excess fabric around a piece of card cut to fit the frame, and secure with stitching behind. Mount the artwork in the frame.

White Apple Blossom

What purer image is there of spring, than that of a tree covered in pretty white or pink blossom? Expressing messages of joy and good tidings, apple blossoms were traditionally used for adorning shawls, headscarves and handkerchiefs given as gifts to close female relations. Expectant new mothers would share their happy news by handing out small gifts trimmed with apple blossom oya. The flowers themselves are symbolic of love and fertility — indeed, it is thought that the ancient Celts would place apple blossom in their bedroom chambers when seeking a night of romance!

You will need

- 1 x 25m (80ft) skein green thread
- 1 x 25m (80ft) skein white thread
- 1 x 25m (80ft) skein yellow thread
- Sewing needle
- Scissors

Skill level 🌸

Time 3–4 hours

Inspiration

Apple blossom appears as the leaves of a tree unfurl in spring and can bloom for as long as one month.

The flower is made of two separate units that are assembled at the end.

STEM

1 Cast on using green thread (see pages 106–107) and make a three-loop base (see pages 108–109).

2 Working from right to left, make three loops to form Round 1 of the stem (see pages 110–111). Fold in half and secure with a knot.

3 Working in the round, make eight rounds of four loops (see pages 112–113). Make the fourth loop on Round 2 in any loop below (see page 116). Cast off (see page 126).

FLAT PETALS

1 Using white thread, cast on in any loop on Round 9 of the stem. Make three loops to form Row 1 of the first petal (see pages 122–123).

2 Your thread should be to the right of your work. Make a reverse knot and continue to work as follows, increasing or decreasing at the end of each row (see pages 114–116):
Row 2: Four loops
Row 3: Five loops
Row 4: Six loops
Row 5: Five loops
Row 6: Four loops

Round 9
Round 8
Round 7
Round 6
Round 5
Round 4
Round 3
Round 2
Round 1

Actual Size

Row 7: Three loops
Row 8: One loop
Cast off.

3 Repeat Steps 1 and 2 to make
an identical petal in the opposite loop
on Round 9 of the stem.

PICOT PETALS

1 Using white thread, cast on in any
remaining loop on Round 9 of the stem.
Make three loops to form Row 1
of the next petal.

2 Your thread should be to the right of your work. Make a
reverse knot and continue to work as follows, and in
the same way as described for making
the flat petals (see page 30):
Row 2: Four loops
Row 3: Five loops

3 For Rows 4 to 6, make picots
on each of four loops in Row 3.
Make two rows of loops, before
making the single picot at the top
(see pages 119). Cast off.

4 Repeat Steps 1 to 3 to make an
identical petal in the remaining loop on Round 9 of the stem.

PICOT CENTRE

1 Start by making a small stem. Cast on
using yellow thread and make a three-loop
base. Working from right to left, make three
loops to form Round 1 of the stem. Fold in
half and secure with a knot. Working in the
round, make a further two rounds of three
loops. For Round 4, make a single picot in
each loop on Round 3. Cast off.

ASSEMBLY

Place the picot centre in the middle of the petals. Make a few neat stitches here
and there to secure the pieces together and then cut any loose ends.

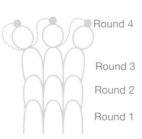

White Apple Blossom Cardigan Trim

There are plenty of ways you can use this delicate-looking blossom, either as a single flower or in little clusters. Try trimming guest towels with a row of blooms for a fresh spring look. Or cover a photograph frame in dozens of blossoms to surround a picture of a newborn baby.

To embellish clothing, such as on this cardigan, simply pin the flowers where you would like them and then stitch into place with a few neat stitches. Here, the buttonholes have been cunningly concealed with the apple blossoms, but the flowers would look equally attractive along the edge of the collar.

Wild Violets

The intense colour of the violet has long been associated with royalty and power. In traditional Turkish culture, oya violets used to trim silk scarves gave an air of comfort and wealth. In terms of oya as the silent voice of Anatolian women, and the messages they conveyed, wild violets were used by young girls to express feelings of loneliness and shyness. Once you have chosen your colours you can interchange them, using dark violet for the outer petals.

You will need

- 1 x 25m (80ft) skein light violet thread
- 1 x 25m (80ft) skein dark violet thread
- 1 x 25m (80ft) skein orange thread
- Sewing needle
- Scissors

Skill level ✿ ✿ ✿
Time 5–6 hours

Inspiration

There are several species of wild violet and all are part of the large genus, *Viola*.

The flower is made of four separate units that are assembled at the end.

OUTER PETALS

1 Start by making the stem. Cast on using light violet thread (see pages 106–107) and make a three-loop base (see pages 108–109).

2 Working from right to left, make three loops to form Round 1 of the stem. Fold in half and secure with a knot (see pages 110–111).

3 Working in the round, make two rounds of four loops (see pages 112–113). Make the additional loop on Round 2 in any loop below (see page 116).

4 With the stem complete, now make the first petal. Working directly onto the stem, and from left to right, make three loops in any loop on Round 3 of the stem, to form Row 1 of the first petal (see page 115).

5 Your thread should be to the right of your work. Make a reverse knot and continue to work as follows, increasing or decreasing at the end of each row (see pages 114–116):
Row 2: Four loops
Row 3: Five loops
Row 4: Six loops
Row 5: Seven loops
Row 6: Eight loops

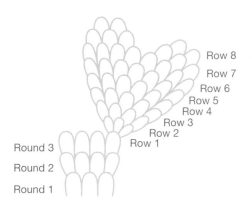

6 To make one side of the petal's heart shape, work from right to left (as you would when making a stem) to make three loops on the right-hand side of the petal (Row 7). Now work in the same way, but from left to right, to make two loops above (Row 8). Cast off (see page 126).

7 To make the opposite side of the heart shape, cast on in the last loop at the left end of Row 5 (see pages 122–123). Repeat Step 6, but work from left to right to make Row 7 (three loops) and from right to left to make Row 8 (two loops). Cast off.

8 Cast on in the opposite loop on Round 3 of the stem and repeat Steps 4 to 7 to make the second petal.

INNER PETALS

1 Start by making the stem. Cast on using dark violet thread and make a three-loop base, leaving a tail of 10cm (4in). Working from right to left, make three loops to form Round 1 of the stem. Fold in half and secure with a knot.

2 Working in the round, make one round of four loops and two rounds of five loops. Make each additional loop on Rounds 2 and 3 by making two loops in any one of the loops below.

3 With the stem complete, now make the first petal the same way as described for making the outer petals (see page 34), working the rows as follows.
Row 1: Three loops
Row 2: Five loops
Row 3: Six loops
Row 4: Seven loops
Row 5: Eight loops

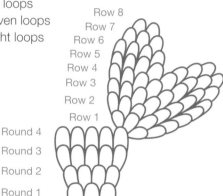

4 To make one side of the petal's heart shape, work from right to left (as you would when making a stem) to make four loops on the right-hand side of the petal (Row 6). Now work in the same way, but from left to right, to make three loops above (Row 7). Then work from right to left to make two loops above (Row 8). Cast off.

5 To make the opposite side of the heart shape, cast on in the last loop at the left end of Row 5. Repeat Step 4, but work from left to right to make Row 6 (four loops), from right to left to make Row 7 (three loops) and from left to right again to make Row 8 (two loops). Cast off.

6 Cast on in any remaining loop on Round 4 of the stem and repeat Steps 3 to 5 to make a second inner petal. Repeat to make the third inner petal.

FAMILY TRADITION

In the large Anatolian family structure of bygone ages, which was very matriarchal, the mother-in-law and any spinster sisters-in-law outranked an incoming bride as head of the home. It would not be unusual in such circumstances for the incoming bride to make a gift of a headscarf trimmed with rich, purple violets to a spinster sister-in-law, highlighting her lonely state and hinting that she might like to marry off and leave the new bride in charge of the household.

PICOT CENTRE

1 Cast on using light violet thread and, leaving a tail of 10cm (4in), make a three-loop base. Working from right to left, make three loops to form Round 1 of the stem. Fold in half and secure with a knot.

2 Working in the round, continue as follows, making the additional loops on each round in any loop below:
Round 2: Four loops
Round 3: Five loops
Round 4: Seven loops

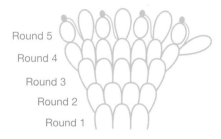

3 For Round 5, make four single picots, alternating with four very large loops (see page 119). Cast off.

SEED-KNOT CENTRE

1 Cast on using orange thread and make a three-loop base. Keep the loops fairly large and a leave tail of 10cm (4in).

2 Working directly into the three loops, make eight knots in each one (see page 118).

ASSEMBLY

Assemble the four units, following one of the two methods described (see pages 124–125). Make sure the inner and outer petals are not aligned with each other, but alternate with each other in the round. You may need to manipulate the pieces a little as you work to make sure that the inner stem sits snugly inside the outer. Make a few neat stitches here and there to secure the pieces together and cut any loose ends.

Actual Sizes

Violet Picture Frame

❦

These rich-coloured spring flowers work beautifully as clusters. You can alternate light and dark sections to create two different flowers and make as many of them as you like. You could use them to create an anniversary posy for a dear friend or relative, simply by stitching them to the top of a measure of green fabric, gathered and tied with a golden ribbon.

Here, a handful of violets has been used to make an attractive embellishment to a silver-plated picture frame. To recreate the look, simply glue the flowers to the corner of a picture frame in an arrangement that suits you. If you don't want to apply glue directly to your flowers, you could stitch them to a length of thin ribbon and tie the ribbon to the frame before inserting the photograph, mount and glass.

ROUGH PROOF.

Summer Charm

Summer is a riot of colour – the bold shades of showy
blooms, rambling climbers and the jewel-like heads of
breezy meadow flowers. Inspiration for the projects in this
chapter comes from white jasmine, pretty forget-me-nots,
oriental lilies and the dainty daisy.

White Jasmine

This scented bloom grows abundantly on shrubs and climbers and is well known for its use in garlands. A common flower in Asia and the Mediterranean, its name comes from the Persian word 'yasmin', which means fragrant flower. In oya, jasmine was traditionally used by young girls or new brides as a trim for brightly printed, summer headscarves and handkerchiefs. Representing grace and elegance, and also sensuality — owing to its alluring and heady scent — the flower itself was often worn in the hair.

You will need

- 1 x 25m (80ft) skein white thread
- Sewing needle
- Scissors

Skill level 🌸
Time 1 hour

Inspiration

Native to tropical and subtropical regions, species of *Jasminum* are grown for the heady fragrance of their delicate flowers.

Stem and petals are made as one single unit.

STEM AND PETALS

1 Cast on using white thread (see pages 106–107) and make a three-loop base (see pages 108–109).

2 Working from right to left, make three loops to form Round 1 of the stem. Fold in half and secure with a knot (see pages 110–111).

3 Working in the round, continue as follows. Make each additional loop in Rounds 4 and 5 in any loop below (see page 116). Make the loops on Round 5 slightly larger:
Round 2: Three loops
Round 3: Three loops
Round 4: Four loops
Round 5: Five loops

Round 4
Round 3
Round 2
Round 1

4 With the stem complete, now make the first petal. Working directly onto the stem, and from left to right, make three loops in any loop on Round 5 of the stem, to form Row 1 of the petal (see page 115).

5 Your thread should be to the right of your work. Make a reverse knot and continue to work the petal as follows, increasing or decreasing at the end of a row (see pages 114–116):

Actual Size

Row 2: Five loops
Row 3: Six loops
Row 4: Five loops
Row 5: Four loops
Row 6: Three loops
Row 7: Two loops

6 You have two options for continuing. The first is to cast off after the last knot on Row 7 of the petal (see page 126) and to cast on with new thread in the next large loop on Round 5 of the stem (see pages 122–123). Alternatively, if you have sufficient thread, you can work down one side of the petal in small loops to continue without casting off the thread (see page 117).

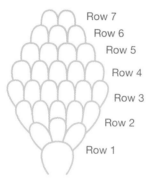

Row 7
Row 6
Row 5
Row 4
Row 3
Row 2
Row 1

7 Either way, follow Steps 4 to 6 to make four more petals – one on each of the remaining loops on Round 5 of the stem. Cast off after the last knot.

8 To finish, tidy up any tails or threads. If you have added a lot of thread, and cannot cut too close to the knots, use the needle tip to nudge the tails in between the loops to make them invisible.

Sugar Jar

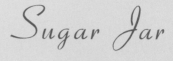

The uses for these elegant flowers are endless. Stitch different coloured blooms onto a plain ribbon when wrapping a gift or arrange them randomly over the surface of a decorative cushion. They also make a perfect addition to a pretty hair garland with other flowers, or scattered across a dining table among real blooms and scented candles.

Everyone loves to invite friends over for tea or coffee. To give the tea tray a lift, why not decorate your sugar jar with oya flowers? First choose three lengths of gauzy ribbon – black and white in this case – to tie around the neck of a jar. Plait the ribbon and stitch on the flowers about 1.5cm (½in) apart. Rather than cut the loose ribbon ends, tie them into a bow around the top of the jar.

Pretty Forget-Me-Nots

When the Turks migrated from Middle Asia to Anatolia, around 500 AD, they brought with them a love of riotous jewel-like colour that is so distinctive to Asia. Bright blue was believed to ward off evil and so the ceilings of the tents of these nomads were swathed with sky-blue and turquoise fabrics. While blue still had protective power, in oya terms, the turquoise and sky-blue forget-me-nots used for trimming headscarves were intended to convey abundance, money and material power.

You will need

- 1 x 25m (80ft) skein turquoise thread
- 1 x 25m (80ft) skein yellow thread
- Sewing needle
- Scissors

Skill level

Time 2 hours

Inspiration

Forget-me-nots are small, five-lobed flowers that grow in blue, pink and white varieties.

The flower is made of two separate units that are assembled at the end.

STEM AND PETALS

1 Start by making the stem. Cast on using turquoise thread (see pages 106–107) and make a three-loop base (see pages 108–109).

2 Working from right to left, make three loops to form Round 1 of the stem. Fold in half and secure with a knot (see pages 110–111).

3 Working in the round, make two rounds of four loops (see pages 112–113). Make the additional loop on Round 2 in any loop below (see page 116). Make the loops on Round 3 slightly larger.

4 With the stem complete, now make the first petal. Working directly onto the stem, and from left to right, make three loops on any loop on Round 3 of the stem to form Row 1 of the petal (see page 115).

5 Your thread should be to the right of your work. Make a reverse knot and continue to work the petal as follows, increasing or decreasing at the end of a row (pages 114–116).
Row 2: Four loops
Row 3: Five loops
Row 4: Four loops
Row 5: Three loops

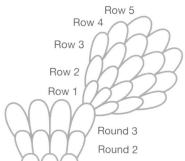

Row 5
Row 4
Row 3
Row 2
Row 1
Round 3
Round 2
Round 1

6 You have two options for continuing. The first is to cast off after the last knot on Row 5 of the petal (see page 126) and to cast on with new thread in the next large loop on Round 3 of the stem (see pages 122–123). Alternatively, if you have sufficient thread, you can work down one side of the petal in small loops to continue without casting off the thread (see page 117).

Forget-me-nots are always seen in little groups and their petal colours vary very slightly. Make a number of these flowers in turquoise and a number using sky-blue to mimic nature's variety.

7 Either way, follow Steps 4 to 6 to make three more petals – one in each of the remaining loops on Round 3 of the stem. Cast off after the last knot.

8 To finish, tidy up any tails or threads. If you have added a lot of thread and cannot cut too close to the knots, use the needle tip to nudge the tails in between the loops to make them invisible.

PICOT CENTRE

1 Start by making a small stem. Cast on using yellow thread and, leaving a tail of 10cm (4in), make a three-loop base. Working from right to left, make three loops to form Round 1 of the stem. Fold in half and secure with a knot.

2 Working in the round, continue as follows, making the additional loops in each round in any loop below:
Round 2: Four loops
Round 3: Five loops

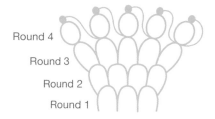

Round 4
Round 3
Round 2
Round 1

3 For Round 4, make a single picot in each of the five loops on Round 3 (see page 119). Cast off when the final picot is complete.

ASSEMBLY

Thread the tail of the picot centre through your needle and pass it through the hollow centre of the flower stem. Make one or two neat stitches to secure the two stems together. Cut off and tidy up any loose ends.

Actual Sizes

Personalised Gifts

These jaunty flowers epitomise summer, with their jewel-like colours. As with the Wild Violets (see pages 34–39), they work brilliantly as clusters with some sky-blue variations nestled among the turquoise ones. You can use them to herald the birth of a summer baby and wish abundance and good fortune upon the baby's future. Attach a bloom to each of a pair of knitted booties or use them to decorate the edges of a Moses basket.

Use your pretty oya forget-me-nots to personalise a gift to a friend or relative. You can stitch them to ribbon that you tie around a box or stick them to a complementary wrapping paper. The forget-me-nots also make lovely additions to envelopes, gift boxes, bags and tags.

Oriental Lily

Lilies of all colours, shapes and sizes feature in oya needle lace and often represent happiness, although they have also been used to denote wealth, innocence and beauty. The shapes of lilies afford a lot of movement, and have a fun and pretty appearance to match these meanings. There are so many varieties of lily that oya versions tend to exercise a certain creative license when it comes to shape, size and colour. In this elegant project, the oriental lily, Lilium 'Stargazer' is the inspiration.

You will need

- 1 x 25m (80ft) skein peach-pink thread
- 1 x 25m (80ft) skein yellow thread
- Sewing needle
- Scissors

Skill level 🌸🌸

Time 3–4 hours

Inspiration

Blooming right through summer, lilies are known for their fragrant perfume and striking colours.

The flower is made of two separate units that are assembled at the end.

OUTER PETALS

1 Start by making the stem. Cast on using peach-pink thread (see pages 106–107) and make a three-loop base (see pages 108–109).

2 Working from right to left, make three loops to form Round 1 of the stem. Fold in half and secure with a knot (see pages 110–111). Working in the round, make a further six rounds of three loops (see pages 112–113).

3 With the stem complete, now make the first petal. Working directly onto the stem, and from left to right, make three loops in any loop on Round 7 of the stem, to form Row 1 of the petal (see page 115).

4 Your thread should be to the right of your work. Make a reverse knot and continue to work the petal as follows, increasing or decreasing at the end of a row (see pages 114–116).
Row 2: Four loops
Row 3: Five loops
Row 4: Six loops
Row 5: Seven loops
Row 6: Six loops
Row 7: Five loops
Row 8: Four loops
Row 9: Three loops
Row 10: Two loops
Row 11: One loop

5 You have two options for continuing. The first is to cast off after the last knot on Row 11 of the petal (see page 126) and to cast on with new thread on the next loop of Round 7 of the stem (see pages 122–123). Alternatively, if you have sufficient thread, you can work down one side of the petal in small loops to continue without casting off the thread (see page 117).

6 Either way, follow Steps 3 to 5 to make two more petals – one in each of the remaining loops on Round 7 of the stem. Cast off after the last knot.

PICOT CENTRE

1 Start by making the stem. Cast on using yellow thread and, leaving a tail of 10cm (4in), make a three-loop base. Working from right to left, make three loops to form Round 1 of the stem. Fold in half and secure with a knot.

2 Working in the round, continue as follows, making the additional loops in Rounds 6, 7 and 8 in any loop below:
Round 2: Three loops
Round 3: Three loops
Round 4: Three loops
Round 5: Three loops
Round 6: Four loops
Round 7: Five loops
Round 8: Six loops

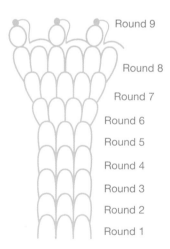

3 For Round 9, alternate three single picots (see page 119) with three long loops. Cast off.

INNER PETALS

1 These petals are smaller than the outer ones and are worked on each of the three long loops on Round 9 of the picot centre. Using peach-pink thread, cast on in any of the long loops on Round 9 of the picot centre. Working from left to right, make three loops to form Row 1 of the petal.

2 Make a reverse knot and continue as follows. (Notice that a six-loop row skips to a four-loop row on the decrease. This is intentional and will help to make a sharp invert shape on the petal):
Row 2: Four loops
Row 3: Five loops
Row 4: Six loops
Row 5: Four loops
Row 6: Three loops
Row 7: Two loops
Row 8: One loop

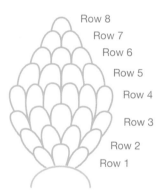

3 As described for making the outer petals, you can either cast off after the last knot on Row 8 and cast on using new thread in the next long loop on Round 9 of the picot centre. Or, if you have sufficient thread, you can work down one side of the petal to move on to the next loop of the stem without casting off.

4 Either way, follow Steps 1 to 3 to make two more petals – one in each of the remaining long loops on Round 9 of the picot centre. Cast off after the last knot.

ASSEMBLY

Assemble the two units, following one of the two methods described (see pages 124–125). Make sure the inner and outer petals are not aligned with each other, but alternate with each other in the round. You may need to manipulate the pieces a little as you work to make sure that the inner stem sits snugly inside the outer. Make a few neat stitches here and there to secure the pieces together and cut any loose ends.

Depending on how you plan to use your lilies, it might be better to leave the tails long when assembling the flowers. For example, if you'd like to attach them to a piece of jewellery, as in the projects on pages 55 and 59, a long tail will prove useful for winding around the cord of a bracelet, necklace or a hairclip.

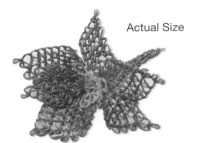

Actual Size

Oriental Lily Necklace

What better way to set off a backless, summer-evening dress or top than with a cluster of lace flowers at the nape of your neck? To make this simple, yet elegant, jewellery you do not need any particular skills or tools. Work with the clasp on the necklace done up and, taking each flower one by one, wind the tail very tightly around the necklace cord (just between where the last pearl meets the clasp). Make a couple of knots to secure each flower in place. Repeat this for any number of flowers, until you have an arrangement you like. Alternatively, you can create your own design by making more flowers and placing them at random in between the beads all around the necklace. These lilies would also make a sweet feature on a matching bracelet, (see page 51).

Dainty Daisy

Daisies feature widely in oya needle lace. The flower has a range of meanings, but is most commonly associated with the purity and innocence of young girls. A Turkish sonnet was written many years ago to honour a bride who wore daisies on her headdress: 'thy bliss shines clear, from the daisy oya in thine hair.' Although the flower may look simple to make, it can take some practice to achieve a uniform look.

You will need

- 1 x 25m (80ft) skein white thread
- 1 x 25m (80ft) skein yellow thread
- Sewing needle
- Scissors

Skill level ✿ ✿ ✿

Time 2 hours

Inspiration

The common daisy, *Bellis perennis*, is native to gardens and fields in Europe, and also grows in the Americas and Australasia.

The flower is made as one single unit, without a stem.

FLOWER CENTRE

1 Cast on using yellow thread (see pages 106–107) and make a five-loop base (see pages 108–109). Your five loops should make a neat, flat circle. This is Round 1 of the flower centre.

2 Continue to make loops around the edge of this circle, drawing the working thread across the top of the loop you have just made before making the knot, just as you would when making a stem (see pages 110–111). Work as follows: increase the loops on Round 2 by making two loops in each loop below (10 loops, see page 116); on Round 3, increase at random intervals to form 14 loops. Cast off once the final loop has been made (see page 126).

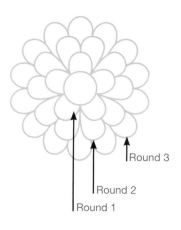

Round 3

Round 2

Round 1

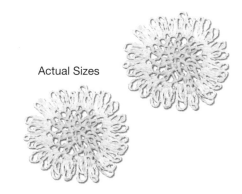

Actual Sizes

If you want to make the hairpin inspiration shown here, be sure to leave a long tail when you cast on for the flower centre, say 10cm (4in).

PICOT PETALS

1 Using white thread, cast on in any loop on Round 3 of the flower centre (see pages 122–123) and work as follows:

Picot round 1: Make 13 single picots, leaving a long loop between each one. (Note that one loop on Round 3 of the flower centre will not have a picot worked into it.)

Picot round 2: Make 15 single picots on the long loops made in Picot round 1, making the additional picots in any long loop below. Cast off.

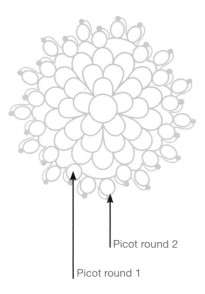

Picot round 2

Picot round 1

Daisy Hairpin

The ultimate meadow flower, the daisy is a frequent choice for embellishment – use them as a feature on a pair of fabric espadrilles or to decorate the yoke on a summer dress or blouse. They also make an impact if used in abundance and sewn on to a cool, white cotton scarf.

Here the daisies sit pretty on a pair of hairpins – perfect for a little girl to match a summery dress. Hairpins are believed to have endured as long as mankind and some decorated with daisies were found during an excavation of the Minoan Palace in Crete. To make these, simply wind the long tail of each daisy around the bend of the hairpin and tie in a double knot very tightly so that it does not slip off. You may glue it if you wish.

Autumn Glory

Pink chrysanthemums, frilly dahlias, the calla lily and salmon begonias provide inspiration for the projects in this chapter. Their soft flower heads, in a range of warm autumnal shades, epitomise the blooms that herald the end of the summer months.

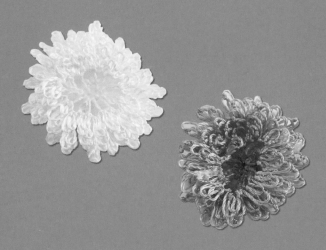

Pink Carnation

In oya needle lace, the carnation is one of the most loved and highest valued of all flowers, with known examples of its use as a trim dating back to around 250 years ago. Historically, carnations have been used to represent a woman's love or affection and, traditionally, gifts trimmed with oya carnations were given to the most respected and closest friends and family members. You can make the leaves for this flower as long as you want.

You will need

- 1 x 25m (80ft) skein green thread
- 1 x 25m (80ft) skein pink thread
- Sewing needle
- Scissors

Skill level 🌸

Time 6–7 hours

Inspiration

Belonging to the *Dianthus* genus, carnations are found in pink, red, white and burgundy varieties.

The flower is made as eight separate units and assembled at the end.

STEM AND LEAVES

1 Start by making the stem. Cast on using green thread (see page 106–107) and make a three-loop base (see pages 108–109).

2 Working from right to left, make three loops to form Round 1 of the stem. Fold in half and secure with a knot (see pages 110–111).

3 Working in the round, make a further seven rounds of three loops (see pages 112–113).

4 With the stem complete, now make the first leaf. Working directly onto the stem, and from left to right, make three loops in any loop on Round 8 of the stem, to form Row 1 of the leaf (see page 115).

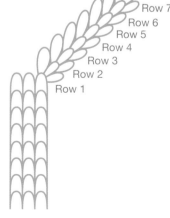

5 Your thread should be to the right of your work. Make a reverse knot and work a further six rows of three loops (see pages 114–115). Make sure that the last loop on each row is slightly larger; this will form the top edge of the leaf.

6 Cast off after the last knot on Row 7 (see page 126) and cast on with new green thread in the opposite loop on Round 8 of the stem (see pages 122–124).

7 Follow Steps 4 and 5 to make a second leaf. Cast off after the last knot. Once complete, the leaves will develop a natural curl.

PETALS

1 Cast on in pink thread, leaving a tail of 10cm (4in), and make a three-loop base. This forms Row 1 of your petal. Your thread should be to the right of your work. Make a reverse knot and work from left to right to form Row 2 of the petal (four loops).

2 For each subsequent row, start again with a reverse knot and work as follows, increasing at the end of each row (see page 116):
Row 3: Five loops
Row 4: Six loops
Row 5: Seven loops
Row 6: Eight loops
Row 7: Nine loops
Row 8: Ten loops

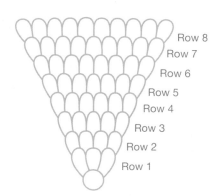

Row 8
Row 7
Row 6
Row 5
Row 4
Row 3
Row 2
Row 1

PICOT PETALS

Finish the petal by making a row of five picot loops (see page 119). These picots vary slightly to the ones in the Oya Techniques section, so follow the diagram below to see where to make the knots and the direction of the thread. Cast off (see page 126).

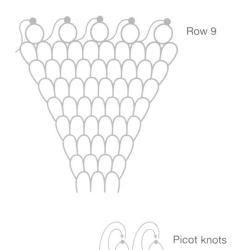

Row 9

Picot knots

ASSEMBLY

Assemble the flower sections, arranging the seven petals at random, and following one of the two methods described (see pages 124–125). Make sure the petals are not aligned with each other, but alternate with each other in the round. Make a few neat stitches here and there to secure the pieces together and cut any loose ends.

Actual Size

Carnation Silk Bag

Carnations are usually made in a large size and make great statement pieces – a lapel pin or brooch, for example. They can also be used to add a personal touch to a treasured item, as with this trousseau purse – a vintage, shantung silk purse, hand-embroidered by a Serbian artist. The pink and green embroidery and feminine nature of the bag suit the carnation in both colour and interpretation of its meaning. To achieve a similar look, leave a long tail at the beginning of your green stem and then thread on a few matching beads; secure with a knot. You can then attach the flower to a jump ring small enough to latch on to the zip of your purse.

Frilly Dahlia

In traditional Turkish culture, after the formal wedding service, a prayer ceremony would be held, during which the bride was expected to place a shawl trimmed with dahlias around her sister-in-law's shoulders. This symbolised peace and understanding between the two women. Today the flower has more widespread meaning, and can be given to express commitment and a lasting bond, among other things.

You will need

- 1 x 25m (80ft) skein yellow thread
- 1 x 25m (80ft) skein purple thread
- Sewing needle
- Scissors

Skill level 🌸🌸

Time 2 hours

Inspiration

Native to Central America, dahlias are cultivated throughout the world and loved for their many vibrant colours.

Each flower is made as a single unit.

FLOWER CENTRE

1 Start by making a short stem that will grow to be the centre of the flower. Cast on using yellow thread (see pages 106–107) and make a three-loop base (see pages 108–109).

2 Working from right to left, make three loops to form Round 1 of the stem. Fold in half and secure with a knot (see pages 110–111).

3 Working in the round, continue as follows. Make additional loops on Rounds 3, 4, 5 and 6 in any loop below (see page 116). Make the loops on Round 6 slightly larger. Cast off once you have made the final loop (see page 126).

Round 2: Three loops
Round 3: Four loops
Round 4: Five loops
Round 5: Seven loops
Round 6: Nine loops

If you want to make the barette inspiration on page 69, be sure to leave a long tail when you cast on, say 10cm (4in).

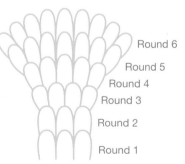

Round 6
Round 5
Round 4
Round 3
Round 2
Round 1

Actual Sizes

PICOT PETALS

1 Using purple thread, cast on in any loop on Round 6 of the stem
(see pages 122–123).

Continue to work in the round as follows:

Picot round 1: Make nine single picots with long loops in between.

Picot round 2: Make 11 pairs of single picots on the long loops made in
Picot round 1, making the additional picot pairs in any long loop below.

Picot round 3: Make 11 pairs of single picots in the long loops made in
Picot round 2.

Picot round 4: Make 12 pairs of single picots in the long loops made in
Picot round 3, making the additional picot pairs in any long loop below.

2 Cast off.

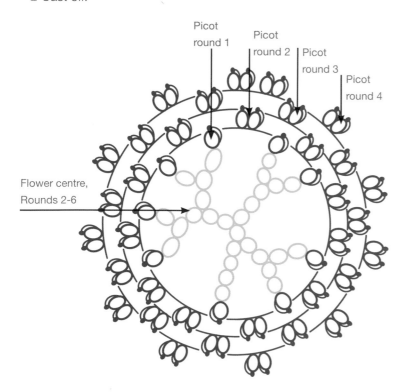

Flower centre,
Rounds 2-6

Picot round 1

Picot round 2

Picot round 3

Picot round 4

Dahlia Hair Barette

These perfectly pretty little flowers are ideal for all kinds of autumn jewellery – you could decorate a brooch pin or a belt buckle in a similar way to this barette, or stitch a number of blooms to a wide band of cotton elastic for a floral wristlet. Try making a number of these flowers in different colour combinations. For a piece to wear in the hair, simply glue dahlias on to the top of a plain barette. Alternatively, if the shape allows, wind the tails of the stems around the barette, secure with a couple of knots and cut off any loose ends.

Calla Lily

We are used to seeing calla lilies at both joyous and solemn events, such as weddings and funerals, where they are chosen for their elegance and purity. In the language of oya, lilies simply represent happiness and are used as trim on the shawls of women who want to announce this to the world.

You will need

- 1 x 25m (80ft) skein green thread
- 1 x 25m (80ft) skein lilac thread
- Sewing needle
- Scissors

Skill level 🌸🌸🌸

Time 7–8 hours

Inspiration

Native to southern Africa, *Zantedeschia aethiopica* is widely cultivated for its elegant blooms.

Each flower is made of three separate units that are assembled at the end.

MAIN STEM AND LEAVES

1 Start by making the main stem. Cast on using green thread (see pages 106–107). Make a three-loop base (see pages 108–109).

2 Working from right to left, make three loops to form Round 1 of the stem. Fold in half and secure with a knot (see pages 110–111).

3 Working in the round, continue as follows (see pages 112–113). Make the additional loops on Rounds 2 and 3 in any loop below:
Round 2: Four loops
Round 3: Five loops
Round 4: Five loops
Round 5: Five loops
Round 6: Five loops
Round 7: Five loops

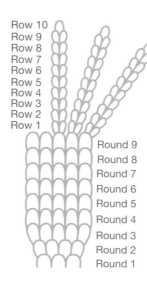

Row 10
Row 9
Row 8
Row 7
Row 6
Row 5
Row 4
Row 3
Row 2
Row 1

Round 9
Round 8
Round 7
Round 6
Round 5
Round 4
Round 3
Round 2
Round 1

Actual Size

Round 8: Five loops
Round 9: Five loops

4 Using the same length of green thread, make the first leaf in any one of the loops on Round 9 of the stem. Work from right to left for Row 1, from left to right for Row 2, and so on, as you would for making Round 1 of a stem (rather than by making a reverse knot). Make the rows as follows and cast off after the final loop (see page 126):
Row 1: Two loops
Row 2: Two loops
Row 3: Two loops
Row 4: Two loops
Row 5: Two loops
Row 6: Two loops
Row 7: Two loops
Row 8: Two loops
Row 9: Two loops
Row 10: One loop

5 Repeat Step 4 to make two more leaves – one on each of two adjacent loops on Round 9 of the stem, so keeping the three leaves close together.

SECONDARY STEM AND LEAF

1 Using green thread, cast on in any one remaining loop on Round 9 of the main stem. Make three loops to form Round 1 of the secondary stem. Fold in half and secure with a knot.

2 Working in the round, make a further six rounds of four loops. Make the additional loop on Round 2 in any loop below (see page 116).

3 With the secondary stem complete, now make the leaf in any one of the four loops on Round 7 of the secondary stem. Make two loops to form Row 1 of the final leaf and continue as follows. Work in the same way as you did for making the first three leaves and cast off after the last loop.
Row 2: Two loops
Row 3: Two loops
Row 4: Two loops
Row 5: Two loops
Row 6: Two loops
Row 7: Two loops
Row 8: One loop

Row 8
Row 7
Row 6
Row 5
Row 4
Row 3
Row 2
Row 1

Round 7
Round 6
Round 5
Round 4
Round 3
Round 2
Round 1

PETALS

1 Cast on using white thread and make a three-loop base. Keep your loops a reasonable size, as they will count as Row 1 of your petal. Your thread should be to the right of your work. Make a reverse knot and continue as follows, increasing and decreasing at the end of a row, as necessary (see pages 114–116):

Row 2: Three loops
Row 3: Three loops
Row 4: Three loops
Row 5: Four loops
Row 6: Six loops
Row 7: Seven loops
Row 8: Nine loops
Row 9: Ten loops
Row 10: Twelve loops
Row 11: Twelve loops
Row 12: Twelve loops
Row 13: Twelve loops
Row 14: Eleven loops
Row 15: Twelve loops
Row 16: Eleven loops
Row 17: Ten loops
Row 18: Nine loops
Row 19: Eight loops
Row 20: Seven loops
Row 21: Seven loops
Row 22: Six loops
Row 23: Five loops
Row 24: Four loops
Row 25: Three loops
Row 26: Three loops
Row 27: Three loops
Row 28: Three loops
Row 29: Two loops
Cast off.

2 Repeat Step 1 to make a second petal.

CENTRE STALK

1 Casting on using white thread and make a three-loop base. Working from right to left, make three loops to form Round 1 of the stem. Fold in half and secure with a knot. Working in the round, make a further nine rounds of three loops.

2 Cast off and join in orange thread for the tip (see pages 122–123).

3 Continue to work in the round as follows, increasing and decreasing in any one loop below, as necessary:

Round 11: Three loops
Round 12: Four loops
Round 13: Four loops
Round 14: Four loops
Round 15: Three loops
Round 16: Two loops
Round 17: One loop

4 Cast off and repeat steps 1 to 3 to make a second stalk.

ASSEMBLY

To make each flower, place a stalk in the centre of a petal with the orange tip at the top. Wrap the base of the petal around the base of the stalk and sew into place using the same thread and a sewing needle. Make sure that you have knotted the end of your thread in the conventional manner. Repeat for the second stalk and petal. Place one lily on each of the stems and use green thread to make a few invisible stitches in and out of the stem to secure the lilies to place (see page 126).

Row 29
Row 28
Row 27
Row 26
Row 25
Row 24
Row 23
Row 22
Row 21
Row 20
Row 19
Row 18
Row 17
Row 16
Row 15
Row 14
Row 13
Row 12
Row 11
Row 10
Row 9
Row 8
Row 7
Row 6
Row 5
Row 4
Row 3
Row 2
Row 1

Round 17
Round 16
Round 15
Round 14
Round 13
Round 12
Round 11
Round 10
Round 9
Round 8
Round 7
Round 6
Round 5
Round 4
Round 3
Round 2
Round 1

Calla Lily 73

Journal Tie

The calla lily is such an elegant bloom, it works best when used sparingly. Turn it into a brooch for a black evening suit or to decorate a favour given at an autumn wedding. Add one to a private journal to give it a personal twist. Make sure your chosen journal is one that has an element to which you can attach your flowers. This diary is secured with twine. Leave a long tail at the beginning of your main stem and then thread this through a needle and use it to attach the lily to the journal, in this case by winding it around the twine. Make a few knots to secure it in place. Alternatively, you could make your own fabric cover for a plain diary and sew the lilies onto the front of it.

Blooming Begonias

Despite their showy flowers in gorgeous colours, begonias are not the best flowers to give as gifts to a lover or spouse. In oya needle lace the begonia is a portentous bloom, representing bad intentions and fortune-seekers. It often carries a warning to tread carefully. Nevertheless a needle-lace begonia makes a beautiful trim for any accessory.

You will need

- 1 x 25m (80ft) skein salmon pink thread
- 1 x 25m (80ft) skein dark peach thread
- 1 x 25m (80ft) skein green thread
- Sewing needle
- Scissors

Skill level ❀

Time 6–7 hours

Inspiration

With as many as 1,400 species, begonias grow in a wide range of vibrant colours.

The flower is made of three separate units that are assembled at the end.

BASE LEAVES

1 Cast on using green thread (see pages 106–107) and make a three-loop base (see pages 108–109). When pulling the tail thread to make the loops, keep the hoop that was on the finger larger than usual. You will be starting two leafy stems from this hoop (see page 77), so it needs to be big enough to accommodate the extra thread.

2 Working from left to right, make three loops to form Row 1 of the first leaf on any one of the base loops you made in Step 1 (see pages 114–115).

3 Your thread should be to the right of your work. Make a reverse knot to start Row 2 of the leaf shape and continue to work the leaf as follows, increasing or decreasing at the end of a row (see page 116).
Row 2: Four loops
Row 3: Four loops
Row 4: Three loops
Row 5: Two loops
Row 6: One loop

4 Cast off (see page 126).

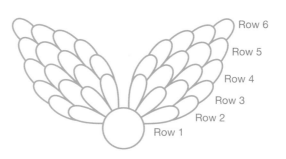

Row 6
Row 5
Row 4
Row 3
Row 2
Row 1

Actual Size

5 Cast on to a second loop on the three-loop base (see pages 122–123) and repeat steps 1 to 4 to make a second leaf.

LEAFY STEMS

1 Make two stems. For the first stem, work directly into the hoop section of the three-loop base. Working from right to left, make three loops to form Round 1 of the stem. Fold in half and secure with a knot (see pages 110–111).

2 Working in the round, make six rounds of four loops (see pages 112–113). Make the extra loop on Round 2 in any loop below (see page 116).

3 Without casting off (unless you are out of thread and need to join a fresh length), now make a small leaf in any loop on Round 7 of the stem. Working from left to right, make two loops to form Row 1 of the leaf and then make a reverse knot, drawing the thread from right to left. Continue as follows:
Row 2: Three loops
Row 3: Four loops
Row 4: Three loops
Row 5: Two loops
Row 6: One loop
Cast off.

4 Cast on in the opposite loop on Round 7 of the stem and repeat Step 3 to make a second leaf.

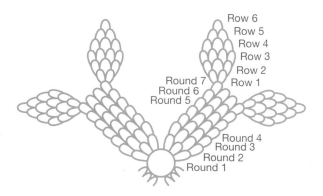

5 Cast on in the last remaining base loop and repeat steps 1 to 4 to make a second leafy stem.

FLOWERS

1 Start by making a short stem. Cast on using salmon-pink thread and make a three-loop base. Working from right to left, make three loops to form Round 1 of the stem. Fold in half and secure with a knot.

2 Working in the round, continue as follows, making the additional loop on Round 2 in any loop below:
Round 2: Four loops
Round 3: Four loops
Round 4: Four loops
Picot round 5: Make four treble picots, keeping the loops very small, but leaving a long loop between each (see pages 119–121).
Picot round 6: Make five treble picots in the long loops made on Round 5, leaving a long loop between each and making the additional treble picot in any long loop below.
Picot round 7: Make five treble picots in the long loops made on Round 6, leaving a long loop between each.

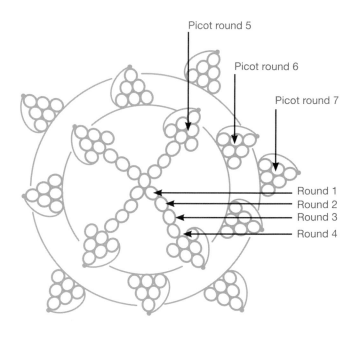

3 Cast off and repeat Steps 1 and 2 to make a second flower.

STAMEN

1 Start by making a very small stem. Cast on using dark peach thread and make a three-loop base. Working from right to left, make three loops to form Round 1 of the stem. Fold in half and secure with a knot.

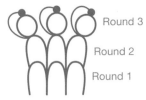

Round 3

Round 2

Round 1

2 Working in the round, make one more round of three loops, followed by a round of single picots. Cast off.

3 Repeat Steps 1 and 2 to make a second stamen.

ASSEMBLY

To assemble each flower, first insert the stem of each stamen into the centre of each flower and make a few neat stitches (see page 126). Then place each flower onto a leafy stem and stitch in place using green thread.

Scented Bag

*This bright bloom is ideal for adorning all
manner of household linens – the corners of
fabric table mats; centred on a table runner;
attached to ribbons for use as napkin ties, or,
as here, as a decoration on a scented bag for your
top drawer or linen cupboard. To make the bag,
you will need a piece of natural linen measuring
approximately 18 x 12cm (7 x 5in). Fold the fabric
in half widthways and wrong sides together and
sew, leaving the top open. Turn right side out and
stitch a number of begonias to the centre of one
side of the pouch before filling with a handful
of dried lavender. Draw the mouth of the pouch
closed with a ribbon, tied in a bow.*

Winter Cheer

What better way to celebrate the winter months, than with the charming blooms that feature in this chapter? Winter roses, elegant chrysanthemums, Mexican shellflowers and a festive poinsettia — big and bold, these are the inspirations for the projects that follow.

Winter Roses

Roses grow all over the world and so are available as cut flowers throughout the year. The rose has long been used to represent love and faith. Many examples remain today of oya roses used as a trim for clothing and scarves that date from the 16th and 17th centuries. Collectively, they all represent lasting love and happiness, yet roses of different colours and varieties have their own language. New brides often wore rambling roses in the early days of their marriage to express their joyous new role in life and love.

You will need

- 1 x 25m (80ft) skein green thread
- 1 x 25m (80ft) skein burgundy thread
- Sewing needle
- Scissors

Skill level 🌸
Time 5–6 hours

Inspiration

Roses are grown worldwide for their range of colours and heady scent.

The flower is made of several units that are assembled at the end.

STEM AND LEAVES

1 Start by making the stem. Cast on using green thread (see pages 106–107) and make a three-loop base (see pages 108–109).

2 Working from right to left, make three loops to form Round 1 of the stem. Fold in half and secure with a knot (see pages 110–111).

3 Work in the round as follows, making the extra loops in Rounds 2 and 4 in any loop below (see page 116):
Round 2: Four loops
Round 3: Four loops
Round 4: Five loops

4 With the stem complete, now make the first leaf. Working directly on the stem, and from left to right, make three loops in any loop on Round 4 of the stem, to make Row 1 of the leaf (see pages 115).

5 Your thread should be to the right of your work. Make a reverse knot and continue to work the leaf as follows, increasing or decreasing at the end of a row (see pages 114–116):
Row 2: Four loops
Row 3: Five loops
Row 4: Six loops
Row 5: Seven loops
Row 6: Eight loops

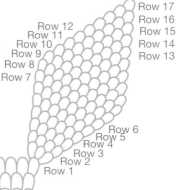

Row 17
Row 16
Row 15
Row 14
Row 13
Row 12
Row 11
Row 10
Row 9
Row 8
Row 7
Row 6
Row 5
Row 4
Row 3
Row 2
Row 1
Round 4
Round 3
Round 2
Round 1

Row 7: Nine loops
Row 8: Ten loops
Row 9: Nine loops
Row 10: Eight loops
Row 11: Seven loops
Row 12: Six loops
Row 13: Five loops
Row 14: Four loops
Row 15: Three loops
Row 16: Two loops
Row 17: One loop
Cast off (see page 126).

6 Cast on, in green, in any other loop on Round 4 of the stem (see pages 122–123) and repeat Steps 4 to 5 twice, to make a second leaf, and then a third. Make sure you space the three leaves at random intervals along Round 4 of the stem.

SMALL PETAL

1 Cast on using burgundy thread and make a three-loop base – this is Row 1 of the petal. As you pull the tail end to draw the hoop to a close, keep it very slightly open – just enough to pass the tip of a needle through. Your working thread should be to the right of your work.

2 Make a reverse knot and continue to work the petal as follows increasing or decreasing at the end of each row:
Row 2: Four loops
Row 3: Five loops
Row 4: Six loops
Row 5: Five loops
Row 6: Four loops
Row 7: Three loops
Row 8: Two loops

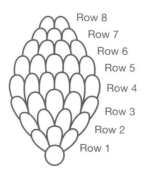

3 Cast off at the top of the petal and repeat Steps 1 and 2 to make a second small petal.

LARGE PETAL

1 Follow the steps for making a small petal, with rows as follows:
Row 1: Three loops
Row 2: Four loops
Row 3: Five loops
Row 4: Six loops
Row 5: Seven loops
Row 6: Seven loops
Row 7: Six loops
Row 8: Five loops
Row 9: Four loops
Row 10: Three loops

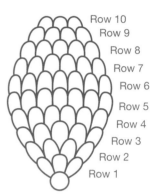

2 Cast off at the top of the petal and repeat Step 1 to make a further six petals.

ASSEMBLY

To make a small flower (yellow flower below), you need two small petals and seven large petals. Arrange the large petals in a round, with the two small petals on top. Use a new thread to stitch through the small hoop at the base of each petal, and use neat stitches to secure them as a flower (see page 126). To make a large flower (burgundy flower below), repeat these steps using eight large petals. As there is no stem on the roses, you simply stitch the centre of the rose to the stem with leaves, ensuring that the leaves show from underneath the rose. Tidy up any straggly ends and cut off any tails.

Actual Sizes

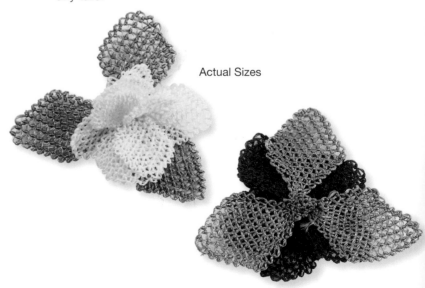

Wedding Roses

─────❧❦❧─────

Big, bold and colourful, oya roses are the ideal choice for all manner of decorations, not least for a white wedding. You could stitch them onto a ring-bearer's cushion for embellishment, or attach them to a ribbon securing a bride's bouquet. They would also make beautiful keepsakes in their own right, given to female guests as favours. Here, they have been used as an alternative to sugar flowers to decorate a simple cake.

Mexican Shellflower

The shellflower grows under a variety of names and colours and, while some are tropical, there are also a number that bloom in wet wintry conditions. Whatever their season, they all carry the peculiar rarity of having three petals. A popular style in oya needle lace is a three-petalled bloom, sometimes referred to simply as 'evening pleasure', which was traditionally used for decorating shawls and headscarves that would be worn by girls on their evening outings, such as to weddings, fairs and visits to neighbours.

You will need

- 1 x 25m (80ft) skein red thread
- 1 x 25m (80ft) skein yellow thread
- 1 x 25m (80ft) skein orange thread
- Sewing needle
- Scissors

Skill level

Time 4 hours

Inspiration

The vibrant Mexican shellflower is also known as a tiger flower.

The flower is made of two separate units that are assembled at the end.

STEM WITH THREE PETALS

1 Start by making the stem. Cast on using red thread (see pages 106–107) and make a three-loop base (see pages 108–109).

2 Working from right to left, make three loops to form Round 1 of the stem. Fold in half and secure with a knot (see pages 110–111).

3 Working in the round, make a further four rounds of three loops (see pages 112–113).

4 With the stem complete, now make the first petal. Working directly onto the stem, and from left to right, make two loops in any loop on Round 5 of the stem, to form Row 1 of the petal (see page 115).

5 Your thread should be to the right of your work. Make a reverse knot and continue to work the petal as follows, increasing or decreasing at the end of a row (see page 114–116):

Row 2: Three loops
Row 3: Four loops
Row 4: Five loops
Row 5: Four loops
Row 6: Three loops
Row 7: Two loops
Row 8: One loop

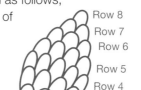

Mexican Shellflower | 89

6 You have two options for continuing. The first is to cast off after the last knot on Row 8 of the petal (see page 126) and to cast on with new thread in the opposite loop on Round 5 of the stem (see pages 122–123). Alternatively, if you have sufficient thread, you can work down one side of the petal in small loops to continue without casting off the thread (see page 117).

7 Either way, follow Steps 4 to 6 to make a second and third petal in the remaining loops on Round 5 of the stem. Cast off after the last knot.

PICOT CENTRE

1 Start by making a stem. Cast on using yellow thread and make a three-loop base. Working from right to left, make three loops to form Round 1 of the stem. Fold in half and secure with a knot.

2 Working in the round, continue as follows, making additional loops on Rounds 5 and 6 in one loop below until you have the required number (see Increasing, page 116):
Round 2: Three loops
Round 3: Three loops
Round 4: Three loops
Round 5: Seven loops
Round 6: Eighteen loops (with every alternate loop made very large).

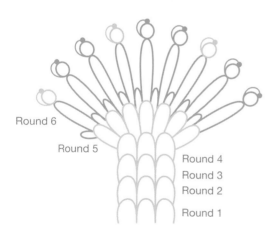

Actual Size

3 As you make the large loops on Round 6, choose three at a roughly equal distance from each other, and top each with a single picot (see page 119). Cast off. Now use orange thread to make single picots at the top of a further six of the long loops on Round 6 – you will have to cast off and cast on for each one.

ASSEMBLY

Use red thread to sew Rows 1–4 of the petals together using small, neat stitches so that they form a triangular cup. Assemble the two flower sections, following one of the two methods described (see pages 124–125).

To make a simple green stem, follow the method used for the Chrysanthemum, but to a smaller scale (see pages 98–99). Make the stem seven rounds of three loops. Then make two leaves, each two loops, three loops, three loops, two loops, one loop.

Mexican Shellflower Earrings

───── ⧖ ─────

Just like the hyacinths that feature in the spring section (see pages 22–25), these Mexican shellflowers are perfect for attaching to pieces that will have movement – earrings, zip pulls, keyrings and such. If you have the patience to make a large number, they make a stunning trim to a headscarf or shawl. To make earrings, use a ready-made set of earring findings (two hooks, two pins). Thread each pin through a small bead and then into the stem end of the flower. Making sure the head of the pin does not pass completely through, but is nestled in the very centre of the flower. Use pliers to bend the end of each pin around the hoop at the bottom of an earring hook. You can use longer pins and more beads if you wish.

Festive Poinsettia

In Turkey, the poinsettia is commonly known as the Atatürk flower, named in honour of the first president of the Republic, Mustafa Kemal Atatürk (1881–1938). This was suggested by botanists of the time and it remains the only flower in the world to have the name of a statesman. The poinsettia was first used in oya needle lace in the 1920s and has no floral meaning other than respect for the memory of Atatürk. Used in adornment and jewellery, the flower carries a certain dignity and elegance.

You will need

- 1 x 25m (80ft) skein green thread
- 1 x 25m (80ft) skein red thread
- 1 x 25m (80ft) skein yellow thread
- Sewing needle
- Scissors

Skill level ❀ ❀

Time 6–7 hours

Inspiration

The poinsettia (*Euphorbia pulcherrima*) is associated with the Christmas season in many cultures.

The flower is made of three separate units that are assembled at the end.

STEM AND LEAVES

1 Start by making the stem. Cast on using green thread (see pages 106–107) and make a three-loop base (see pages 108–109).

2 Working from right to left, make the three loops to form Round 1 of the stem. Fold in half and secure with a knot (see pages 110–111).

3 Working in the round (see pages 112–113), continue as follows. Make the additional loops on Rounds 4 and 5 in one loop below (see page 116). Make the loops on Round 5 slightly larger than the ones in previous rounds.
Round 2: Three loops
Round 3: Three loops
Round 4: Four loops
Round 5: Five loops

4 With the stem complete, now make the first leaf. Working directly on the stem, and from left to right, make two loops in any loop on Round 5 of the stem to form Row 1 of the leaf (see page 115).

5 Your thread should be to the right of your work. Make a reverse knot and continue to work the leaf as follows, increasing or decreasing at the end of a row (see pages 114–116):

Row 18
Row 12
Row 11
Row 10
Row 9
Row 8
Row 7
Row 6
Row 5
Row 17
Row 16
Row 15
Row 14
Row 13
Row 4
Row 3
Row 2
Row 1
Round 5
Round 4
Round 3
Round 2
Round 1

Row 2: Three loops
Row 3: Four loops
Row 4: Five loops
Row 5: Six loops
Row 6: Seven loops
Row 7: Eight loops
Row 8: Nine loops
Row 9: Ten loops
Row 10: Nine loops
Row 11: Eight loops
Row 12: Seven loops
Row 13: Six loops
Row 14: Five loops
Row 15: Four loops
Row 16: Three loops
Row 17: Two loops
Row 18: One loop
Cast off.

6 Using green thread, cast on in the next large loop on Round 5 of the stem (see pages 122–123). Repeat steps 4 to 5 to make a second leaf. Make three more leaves in the same way in the remaining large loops on Round 5 of the stem.

Actual Size

SIX-PETAL SECTION

1 Start by making the stem. Cast on using red thread and make a three-loop base, leaving a tail of 10cm (4in). Working from right to left, make three loops to form Round 1 of the stem. Fold in half and secure with a knot.

2 Working in the round, continue as follows, making the additional loops in each round in one loop below. Make the loops on Round 5 slightly larger:
Round 2: Three loops
Round 3: Four loops
Round 4: Five loops
Round 5: Six loops

3 With the stem complete, now make the first petal. Working directly on the stem, and from left to right, make three loops in any loop on Round 5 of the stem to form Row 1 of the petal (see page 116).

Row 3
Row 2
Row 1

Round 5
Round 4
Round 3
Round 2
Round 1

Row
Row 9
Row 8
Row 7
Row 6
Row 5
Row 4

4 Your thread should be to the right of your work. Make a reverse knot and continue to work the petal as follows, increasing or decreasing at the end of a row:
Row 2: Three loops
Row 3: Four loops
Row 4: Five loops
Row 5: Six loops
Row 6: Five loops
Row 7: Four loops
Row 8: Three loops
Row 9: Two loops
Row 10: One loop
Cast off.

5 Using red thread, cast on in the next loop on Round 5 of the stem. Repeat steps 3 to 4 to make a second petal. Make four more petals in the same way in the remaining loops on Round 5 of the stem.

FIVE-PETAL SECTION

1 Still using red thread, follow the method described for making the six-petal section and make a stem as follows. Make the loops on Round 5 slightly larger:

Round 1: Three loops
Round 2: Three loops
Round 3: Three loops
Round 4: Four loops
Round 5: Five loops

2 Continue to follow the method described for making the six-petal section to make a petal in each loop on Round 5 of the stem, working as follows:

Row 1: Three loops
Row 2: Four loops
Row 3: Five loops
Row 4: Four loops
Row 5: Three loops
Row 6: Two loops
Row 7: One loop
Cast off.

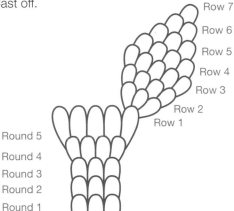

ASSEMBLY

Assemble the three sections, following one of the two methods described (see pages 124–125). Make sure the petals of the two flower sections are not aligned with each other, but alternate with each other in the round. You may need to manipulate the pieces a little as you work, to make sure the inner stem sits snugly inside the outer stem. Make a few neat stitches here and there to secure the pieces together. Once you have assembled the flower, use yellow thread and a sewing needle to work five or six seed knots at the centre of the flower (see page 118). Make sure to wind the thread around the needle three times instead of the usual twice.

Poinsettia Brooch

Most often associated with Christmas, the poinsettia is very versatile when it comes to festive decorations. Twine some black, red and green ribbon around a wreath base, add some holly and place your poinsettia among the leaves for a seasonal door wreath. Wrap a poinsettia around the cord of a necklace of black beads to complement your elegant outfit for Christmas lunch. To make an elegant brooch, simply place a basic brooch pin beneath the stem of your flower and use a needle to wind the thread on securely. Make sure the poinsettia is fixed firmly and does not droop before fastening off.

Elegant Chrysanthemum

The chrysanthemum is the birth flower of November and in Turkish the name kasimpati, translates as 'November and now'. The flower symbolises many things — besides joy and optimism, it also represents hope. It is such a bright, cheerful and sunny bloom in the midst of winter, so these attributes describe it perfectly. In oya needle lace, the colours of the flowers can be interpreted as having meaning too. Red chrysanthemums are used to express a silent wish or hope and white chrysanthemums mean faithfulness.

You will need
- 1 x 25m (80ft) skein green thread
- 1 x 25m (80ft) skein white thread
- 1 x 25m (80ft) skein yellow thread
- Sewing needle
- Scissors

Skill level 🌸
Time 3–4 hours

Inspiration

Chrysanthemum flowers take various forms, including daisy-like and pompom blooms.

The flower is made of two separate units that are assembled at the end.

STEM AND LEAVES
1 Start by making the stem. Cast on using green thread (see pages 106–107) and make a three-loop base (see pages 108–109).

2 Working from right to left, make three loops to form Round 1 of the stem. Fold in half and secure with a knot (see pages 110–111).

3 Continue to work in the round as follows (see pages 112–113), making the additional loops on Rounds 3 and 5 in any loop below (see page 116).
Round 2: Three loops
Round 3: Four loops
Round 4: Four loops
Round 5: Five loops
Round 6: Five loops

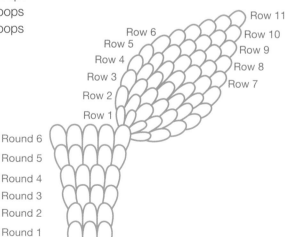

4 With the stem complete, now make the first leaf. Working directly on the stem, and from left to right, make four loops in any loop on Round 6 of the stem to form Row 1 of the leaf (see page 115).

5 Your thread should be to the right of your work. Make a reverse knot and continue to work the leaf as follows, increasing or decreasing at the end of a row (see pages 114–116):
Row 2: Five loops
Row 3: Six loops
Row 4: Seven loops
Row 5: Seven loops
Row 6: Six loops
Row 7: Five loops
Row 8: Four loops
Row 9: Three loops
Row 10: Two loops
Row 11: One loop

6 You have two options for making the next leaf. The first is to cast off after the last knot on Row 11 (see page 126) and to cast on with new thread in the next loop on Round 6 of the stem (see pages 122–123). Alternatively, if you have sufficient thread, you can work down one side of the leaf in small loops to move on to the next loop of the stem without casting off the thread. (see page 117).

7 Either way, follow Steps 4 to 6 to make three more leaves – one in each of the remaining loops on Round 6 of the stem. Cast off after the last knot.

FLOWER CENTRE

1 Start by making a short stem. Cast on using white thread and make a three-loop base. Working from left to right, make three loops to form Round 1 of the stem. Fold in half and secure with a knot.

2 Working in the round, continue as follows, making the additional loops on Round 4 in any loops below. Make the loops on Round 4 slightly larger:
Round 1: Three loops
Round 2: Three loops
Round 3: Three loops
Round 4: Five loops

Round 4
Round 3
Round 2
Round 1

DIFFERENT SIZES

Like other similar oya flowers consisting of mainly picot rounds, chrysanthemums are one of the most flexible in size and shape. It is very easy for you to reduce or increase the number of rounds or the number of picots on each round: if you look at the schematic you can decide where to do this. Alternatively you can make fewer and smaller loops on your last stem row, which will greatly reduce the spread of the flower. This is a good time for you to try your hand at adapting your own oya flowers by looking at the real ones and trying to imitate their varying, natural shapes. If you allow yourself to step outside of the restraints of rows and numbers and let your thread and needle flow freely you may surprised at the flowers you can create. After all, every single flower in nature is unique and 'imperfect'.

Actual Sizes

PICOT PETALS

Still using white thread, cast on in any loop on Round 4 of the flower centre (see pages 122–123) and make five single picots, leaving a long loop between each one, and making the additional picot in any loop below. Work two more rounds of five single picots, with five long loops between. Cast off.

Round 8: Make six single picots in the long loops made on Round 7, making the additional picot in any long loop below and leaving long loops between.
Round 9: Make eight double picots in the long loops made on Round 8, making the additional double picots in any long loop below and leaving long loops between.
Round 10: Make eleven treble picots in the long loops made on Round 9, making the additional treble picots in any long loop below and leaving long loops between.
Round 11: Make thirteen treble picots in the long loops made on Round 10, making the additional treble picots in any long loop below and leaving long loops between. Cast off to complete the flower.

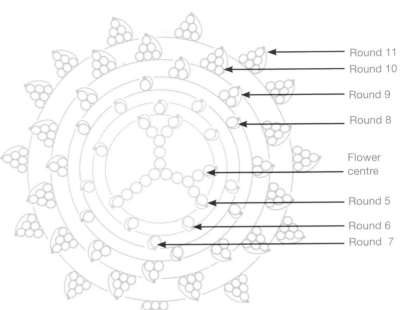

Round 11
Round 10
Round 9
Round 8
Flower centre
Round 5
Round 6
Round 7

Elegant Headband

Chrysanthemums are striking blooms that look great teamed with any outfit. Use a single flower to make a brooch or cocktail ring, or stitch a cluster onto a fabric belt or headband. To embellish a headband, it is best to choose one made in elastic or with a fabric covering, as the flowers can be stitched directly onto that. If you have a plastic Alice band, make each flower with a 10cm (4in) tail when casting on. This can simply be wound around the headband and glued in place to secure.

Oya Techniques

Follow these step-by-step instructions as you progress
through each project in the seasonal chapters.
From making your very first loops to assembling
the separate units that complete a bloom,
everything you need is at your fingertips.

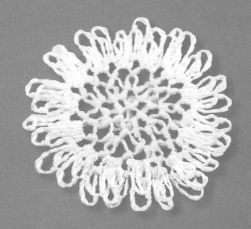

Getting Started

Over the following pages, you will learn the basic steps required for making beautiful needle lace flowers. The methods are easy to follow and the techniques fairly repetitive. It is good practice to master the basic techniques before attempting to make any of the flowers. That way, your work will be controlled and consistent.

If you crochet or make lace, you will be familiar with both working on a very small scale and manipulating fine thread, so this new craft may come more easily to you than it will to those with no experience at all. Either way, there is no doubt that a little practice will lead to some rewarding creations.

Whatever it is you are making – a flower, a leaf or a stem – you start in the same way, with a simple base made of two, three, or more loops (see pages 108–109). With the base complete, you build up your design, working from left to right for some techniques and from right to left for others. It is important to note that the instructions should be carried out as demonstrated here, whether you are left- or right-handed. Left-handed people simply hold the needle in their left hand, but do not alter the direction of work.

Ideally, flowers are made using as few lengths of thread as possible. (When you come to the projects, you will see that several metres might be involved). Keeping the number of added threads to a minimum is preferable, because each new thread introduces a knot that could easily come undone and another tail that needs weaving in on completion – because you are working on such a small scale, this could be unsightly. Having said that, for the purposes of practising the basic techniques, and in order to get to grips with the craft, it is a good idea to start with a shorter length of thread. At first you may experience the thread twisting and knotting together, so keep it short enough to avoid this, say 80cm (30in) long. After sufficient practice controlling the thread and making loops and knots, you can leave the thread as long as you like.

Casting On

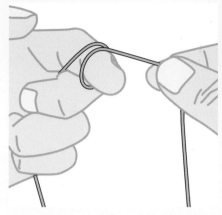

1 Thread the needle as you would for sewing; do not knot either end of the thread. Leave the short end of the thread hanging from the needle and work with the long end of the thread. Leaving a sufficient length – 5–7cm (2–3in) – wind the thread twice around the index finger of your left hand to form two hoops.

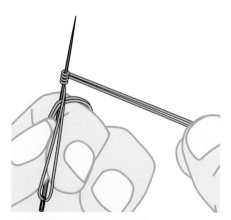

5 Now hold all threads firmly as you push the needle through the hoops on your finger and through the twist of thread on the needle. Pull the needle through gently and slowly.

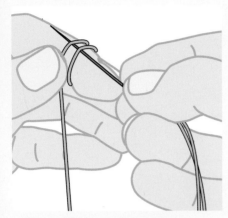

2 Keeping the thread reasonably tightly wound around your finger, guide the tip of the needle under and through the two hoops, but do not pass it all the way through yet.

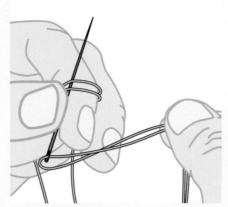

3 With the needle still under the two hoops, and held firmly in your left hand, grasp the two threads emerging from the eye of the needle in your right hand, and pull them gently to the right.

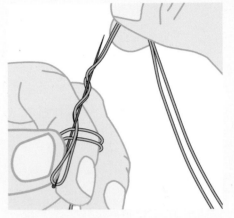

4 Wrap both threads in your right hand around the stem of needle twice, in an anti-clockwise direction. You will repeat this wrapping motion every time you make a knot.

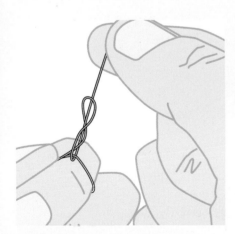

6 As you pull the thread, the hoop nearest your fingertip will slip off the finger naturally and, as a knot forms, you'll see the thread make a figure-of-eight shape.

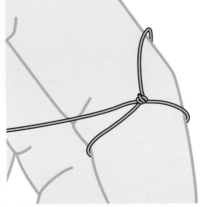

7 Now pull the thread more tightly so that it forms a neat and secure knot on the loop that remains on your index finger. You have made your first knot!

The thread is slippery but sturdy so do not be afraid to pull as firmly as you can to secure a tight knot. Otherwise the knot may loosen.

A Simple Base

The instructions that follow are for a three-loop base, because the majority of projects in this book use a three-loop base on which to build a stem, leaf or petal. Should any stage in a project require fewer or more loops, simply repeat Steps 1 to 3 the required number of times. To start, you will have the first knot attached to a hoop on your finger (see pages 106–107). There will be a short length of thread to the left (tail thread) and the threaded end to the right (working thread). You will also be working with the two threads at the eye of the needle (needle threads – see page 126 for a complete list of oya terminology).

Three-loop Base

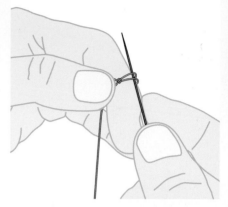

1 Keeping the first knot in place, wind the working thread around the index finger again and repeat Steps 2 to 7 of Casting On to make a second knot. Keep the thread in check using your fingers, which should be slightly curled.

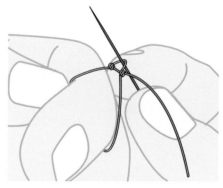

5 As you work, use the tip of the needle to nudge the loops up into good arches. Make good use of the needle and your fingers.

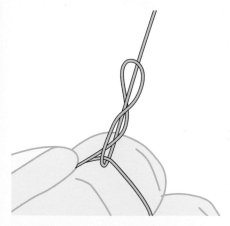

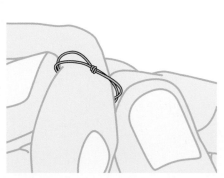

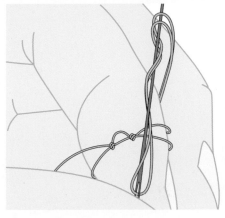

2 Once you have wound the thread around the needle and pushed the needle through, hold the first knot firmly as you pull tightly to make a second knot. If you don't pull at the thread several times quite boldly the knot will loosen.

3 Keep the knots close enough alongside each other to form a neat arch, as shown, and adjust this loop manually before giving a final tug to tighten the second knot completely. This loop between the two knots is the lynchpin of oya!

4 Now repeat Steps 1 to 3 to make a second loop, and then a third. You will have made four knots and three loops in total. Don't worry how tight you tug on the thread once you have formed a loop, it should not break as you tighten the knot.

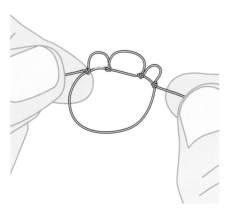

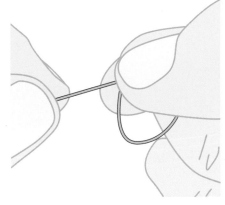

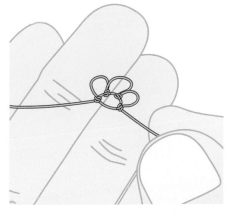

6 Your hoop will look like this once it is off your finger. Ideally it should be a little smaller than this, but that will come with practice.

7 Holding the hoop with the knots and three loops in place with your right hand, pull to the side with the tail end of the thread – firmly!

8 You will have three pretty, equally sized little loops. These are sitting very tightly now. Do not be afraid that they will become loose; they won't.

Making the First Round

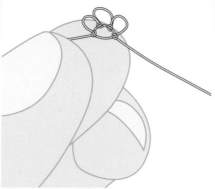

1 Make a three-loop base (see pages 106–109). These loops will barely be noticeable once the stem is formed and are therefore not counted as a round when following a schematic for a project.

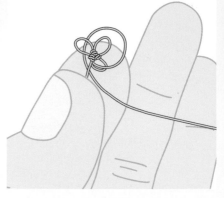

2 Working from right to left, draw the working thread (that is, the thread coming from the last knot you made) across to the left in an arch above your first loop and hold it firmly in your left hand.

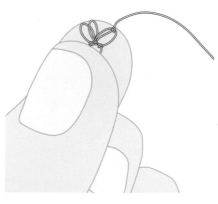

6 As you tighten the knot, a loop will form to the right of your first base loop (this will sit above the base loop once you begin to work in the round). Adjust the size as necessary before tightening the knot completely.

THE ROLE OF THE ARCHED THREAD

When working from right to left, the arched thread that you make at the start of each new knot is the tightrope of oya needle lace. It needs to be consistent and straight in order to provide the security for each knot. Later, when you start to make leaves and petals, you will see an elongated arch used in a similar way when working from left to right (see page 115).

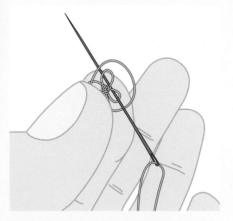

3 Push the needle into the loop and under the arched thread, but do not push it all the way through just yet.

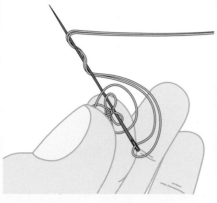

4 Wrap the two threads from the eye of the needle around the stem of the needle twice, anti-clockwise.

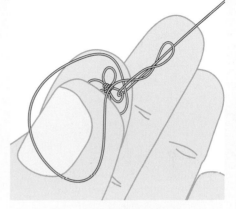

5 Pull the needle through gently. The thread will form a figure-of-eight shape just before the knot tightens.

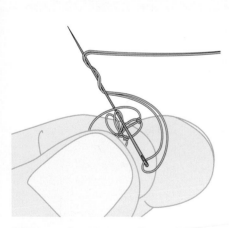

7 Still working from right to left, repeat Steps 2 to 6 to make a second and then a third loop directly into the three-loop base.

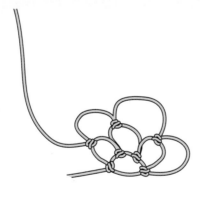

8 You will have a new row of three loops with your working thread waiting on the left. This will become Round 1 of your stem.

The slower you pull the needle through to form a knot, the more smoothly you will be able to create your first loops. Working too fast may result in the thread twisting and knotting on itself. At the same time, take care not to get the tail end caught in your work. If you do not need a long tail for your project, cut it slightly shorter to work more comfortably.

Making Subsequent Rounds

If your stem loops are too large, they will make it difficult to hide the stems of any other pieces that might be used when assembling a flower.

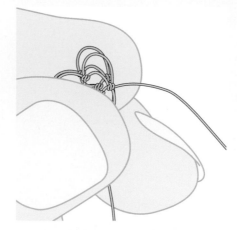

1 Taking the piece you made on pages 110–111, start by folding the work in half vertically, so that the first and last loops you made align with one another. They should overlap.

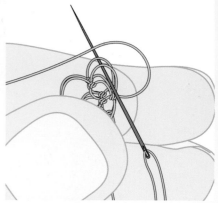

2 Draw the working thread (from the last knot you made) in an arch above the work and hold firmly in your left hand. Now pass the needle through the first and last loops on Round 1.

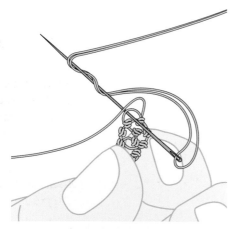

6 Always pass the needle through the loop and under the arched thread before wrapping the two threads from the eye of the needle, twice, in an anti-clockwise direction around the stem of the needle.

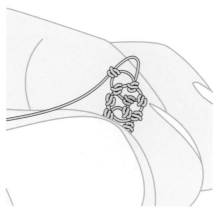

7 Every time you make a knot, the thread will form a figure-of-eight shape just as you tighten the knot. The new loop will form between the last knot that you made and your new knot to the right.

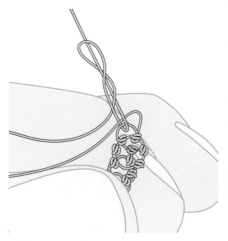

8 If you tug slightly to the left as you pull the thread through, the loop will form cleanly. Continue working in the round until your stem reaches the required height. Try and keep all loops small and equal in size.

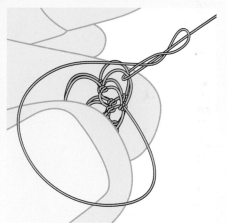

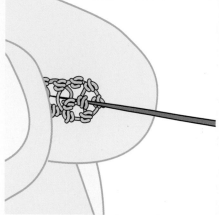

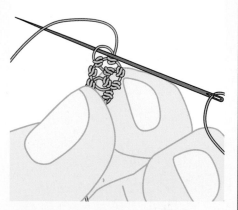

3 When making this knot, allow it to form without a loop by tugging the thread to the right. This will fasten the sides of the stem together to form the conical tip. Any loop that forms will be small and inconsequential.

4 If you poke the tip of your needle inside the centre of your stem, you will be able to see that it is hollow. This is important when it comes to assembling a flower, since inner stems often sit inside outer stems.

5 Now follow Steps 2 and 6 of Making the First Round (see pages 110–111) to work in the round. Always make sure that the working thread is arched above your work before pushing the needle through.

9 The finished stem should look something like this. If your next step is to add leaves or petals in the same colour, do not cast off or cut the thread, but work directly onto the stem, page 115).

MAKING LARGER LOOPS

You can make the loops on the final round slightly larger, by holding the loop that is about to form with your thumb and controlling the knot. This will give you larger loops on which to work petals or leaves.

STEMS OF DIFFERENT SIZES

To increase the number of loops in order to make the stem larger, you make two loops inside any one of the loops in the round below (see page 116). If you simply need to have more loops in order to create a particular number of leaves or petals, then do this on the final round only. If you need to make a smaller stem, start with two loops instead of three.

Making a
Leaf or Petal

Leaves and petals are all made using the same methods, with different shapes achieved by adjusting the number of loops on each row. There are two options available to you. The first is to make individual pieces with long tails, which can then be threaded through a hollow stem for assembly. The second is to work directly onto a stem that you have already made. If adding directly to a stem, start with the leaves (if relevant), as you will not have to cut the thread after the last knot on the stem (see pages 110–113). Whichever way you work, the majority of your loops will be made by working from the left to the right.

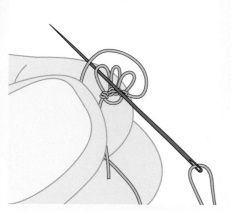

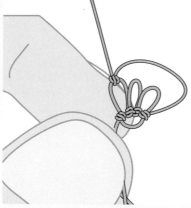

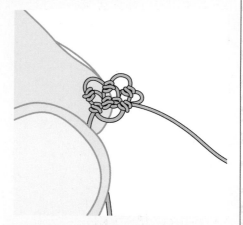

1 Cast on and make a simple base of two, three or more loops (see pages 106–109). Your working thread will be to the right, after the last knot made. Draw it to make an arch, not just above the next loop to the left, but above all the loops. Push the needle through the first loop you made and under the arched thread.

2 Make a knot in the first loop you made in the normal way, to secure the arched thread in place. This is called a reverse knot. Unlike when making a stem (see pages 110–113), the simple base that you make to start a leaf or petal – whether of two, three or more loops – will also form its first row.

3 Continue to work from left to right, arching the working thread over each loop in turn, and inserting the needle through the loop and under the reverse knot thread and under the working thread, before making a knot in the usual way.

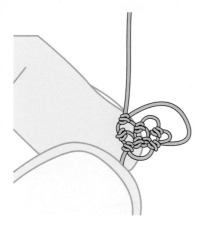

4 Once you reach the end of the row and have made your final knot, draw your working thread all the way across from right to left again, to make a new reverse knot. You can then continue to work the next row of a schematic in the same way.

YOUR TIGHTROPE

The arched thread made by the reverse knot offers a solid framework on which to build a leaf or petal. It needs to be kept taut, to prevent the work fanning out as you build each subsequent row. But it should not be so short that it makes your work curve inwards as you proceed. If the arched thread is too loose or too big, it will leave some excess on its bend at the right-hand side of your work. Subsequently it will form a loop when the final knot holds down the arched thread.

WORKING DIRECTLY ONTO A STEM

If you are adding a leaf or petal to a stem, start by making the required number of loops for Row 1 of the leaf or petal in just one loop in the last round of the stem. Work from left to right, draw the working thread across the top of each loop before wrapping and pushing the needle through. With the working thread to the right of the last knot made, you can then proceed by making a reverse knot and following the instructions for working Row 2 and any subsequent rows.

Increasing

In order to achieve the different petal and leaf shapes, a project may require you to increase or decrease the number of loops on a given row of your work. The technique involves adding one or more loops to either (or both) ends of the work. Note that exactly the same techniques work for increasing or decreasing the width of a flower stem.

WHICH SIDE?

When increasing or decreasing on subsequent rows of a leaf or petal, it is best to do so on the same side each time. This will give a more uniform look. However, there may be times when the shape of a piece is becoming unbalanced and you may chose to increase or decrease on the opposite side for a few rows – it is up to you. If you need to increase by two loops on any row, it makes sense to do so by one loop at each end.

1 To increase a row by one loop at the left-hand side, make a reverse knot as you would for making the next row of loops on a petal and make the first loop as usual. Then make a second loop (still in the first loop below) in the same way.

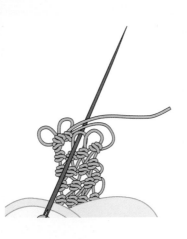

2 To increase at the right-hand side, make two loops in the last loop on the previous row. This piece now has a width of five loops.

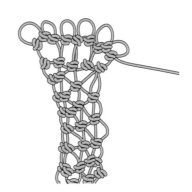

Decreasing

1 To decrease at the left-hand side, make your reverse knot. Instead of making the first loop of the next row in the last loop of the row below, do so in the second loop of the row below. Once the knot is tight, the decrease will form a gentle curve rather than a sharp decrease.

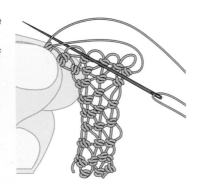

2 To make a decrease on the right, work the row to the second to last loop on the row below and finish here. You will achieve a gentle, even narrowing of your shape.

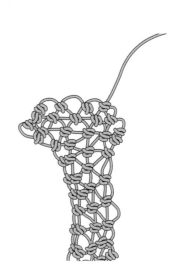

Working Down One Side

After finishing a leaf or petal, if you have sufficient thread on your needle to make the next one, you can work down one side of the petal or leaf just made, in order to move seamlessly on to the next. Once you gain experience, it is ideal to have as few cast-offs as possible in a single flower, as they require cutting the thread very close to the knot (a problem if you have not properly tightened your knots) and joining in new lengths of thread, which makes for extra tidying up (see pages 122–123).

Once a petal or leaf is complete, with a final knot on the last row, do not cast off. One side of the work is likely to be almost imperceptibly more 'frilly' than the other side – usually the right-hand side, because that is where the bend of the reverse knot occurs and may stick out a little like a small rounded loop. This presents a beautiful edge and so it is preferable that you work down the opposite edge (usually the left-hand side) to balance that 'frilly' appearance.

Working the Left Side

1 The last knot you made will be at the top of the petal or leaf. Turn the work on its side and work from right to left, as you would if working in the round (see pages 112–113).

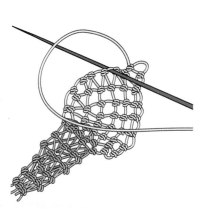

2 As you make the loops along the side of the petal or stem, pull the thread upwards instead of to the side for a perfect loop.

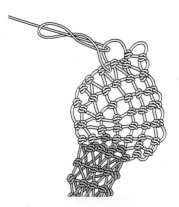

3 Keep the loops small and neat. They should be almost invisible, yet form a pretty frill on the edge. Too obvious or too large and they may then spoil the shape of the petal you want to achieve.

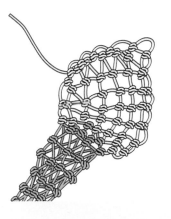

4 As you reach the base make a knot close to next loop on the stem and start the next petal.

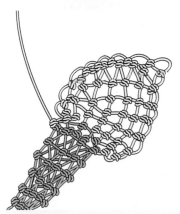

Making a Seed Knot

There will be times when you need to make a simple knot without a loop, either to create a decorative element in your flowers, or to skip a loop altogether.

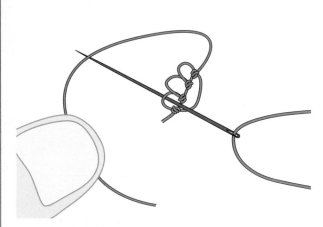

1 To make seeded flower centre, start by making the required number of base loops in the conventional manner (see page 108–109). Draw the working thread above the last loop you made – from right to left.

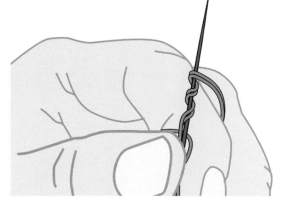

2 Push the needle through the base loop and under the arched thread. Instead of wrapping the working thread around the needle twice, wrap it around the needle three times.

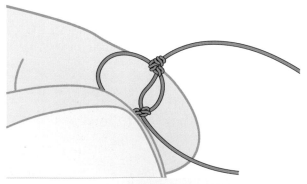

3 Pull the working thread all the way through the base loop. A knot will start to form. Once tightened, push the knot to the side of the loop, to make room for other knots.

4 Work as many knots as you need to fill up the loop and progress to the next, until all base loops have been treated in the same way. As they increase in number, these slightly larger knots will resemble seeds.

Making Picots

This technique is perfect for making frilly stamens or petal edges and involves working a double loop. You can make the loop as tall as you like and can repeat the process for any number of rows, always finishing with a single picot.

Making a Single Picot

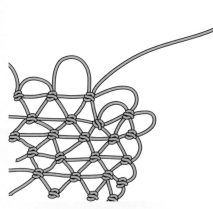

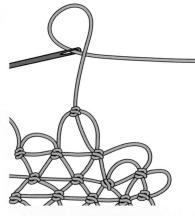

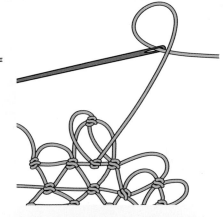

1 For a single picot, make a loop that is very slightly taller than usual.

2 Keeping the working thread high and straight, make a knot right in the centre of the loop you have just made. Work in the normal way.

3 Now make a knot at the centre of the base of the same loop. Again, make sure the thread is standing completely parallel to the loop. This forms the 'frilly' picot loop.

Making a Double Picot

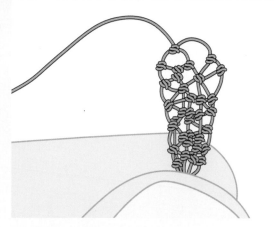

1 In this example, the technique is used for making a frilly stamen. When making a stem (see pages 110–113), work so that the loops on the final row are intentionally larger.

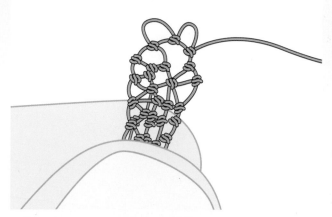

2 Working from left to right, make two loops on any one loop on the stem, in exactly the same way as you would if adding a leaf or petal directly to the stem (see page 115).

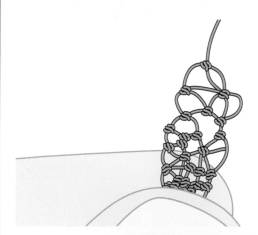

5 Now make a knot right at the centre of the loop you have just made. You will have created a bend in the vertical thread in the process. Note that there is no reverse knot or loop-making here.

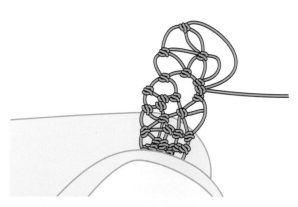

6 From the last knot made, go all the way down to the first row and make a second knot, right beside the last knot made in Step 2. You will have a long picot loop arching around and down.

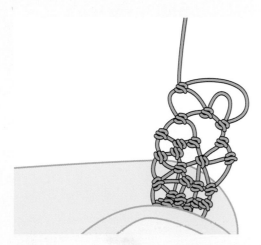

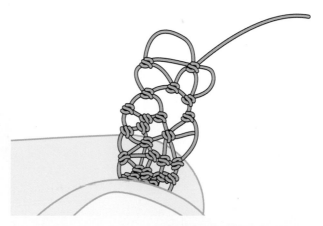

3 Draw the working thread over the two loops you have just made and make a reverse knot (see pages 114–115). While the reverse knot thread needs to be taut for making leaves and petals, it can afford to be looser here.

4 Working from left to right, make a new loop above. To do this, draw the working thread across to the top of the two loops you made in step 2, and wrap the needle threads in the usual way. Your working thread is now to the right of the knot you have just made.

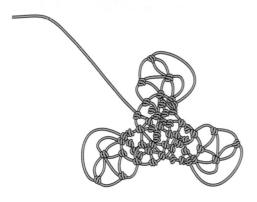

7 Repeat steps 2 to 6 on each of the large loops on your stem as required by the project. This method is used for making frilly flowers, such as the Elegant Chrysanthemum, pages 98–103.

PICOT ROUNDS

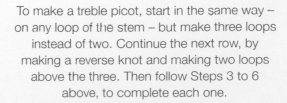

When working several consecutive rounds of picots, make sure you leave a length of thread between each one. Your next round of picots will be made directly onto these lengths.

TREBLE PICOTS

To make a treble picot, start in the same way – on any loop of the stem – but make three loops instead of two. Continue the next row, by making a reverse knot and making two loops above the three. Then follow Steps 3 to 6 above, to complete each one.

Adding New Thread

While any given project is in progress there may be times when your working thread begins to run out and you need to cast on new thread in order to continue. It is a good idea to do this before the working thread becomes too short to manipulate comfortably. It is also a good idea to get to the end of a round or row — any row and any end. The instructions given are shown using two different colours for ease of reference. The colours of your thread will depend on your project.

How to Add Thread

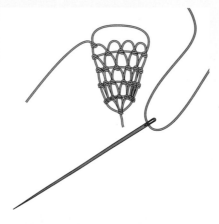

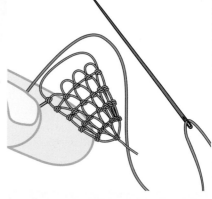

1 Work towards the end of a row, making sure you have a reasonable length of working thread. Make your last knot, in this case a reverse knot, and unthread the needle. Thread your needle with new thread and align the tail end of this with the tail of the working thread.

2 Hold your work in your left hand, making sure you are holding the tail end of both threads firmly between your thumb and index finger.

CASTING ON MID-PROJECT

There will be times when you have to cast on mid-project (e.g., when adding a petal of a different colour to a completed loop of a stem). In these instances, you will not have an existing working thread with which to weave in the new thread. When doing so, follow the same steps as given here, simply without the old working thread. Leave a short tail to enable you to make a very tight knot and trim neatly once the piece is complete.

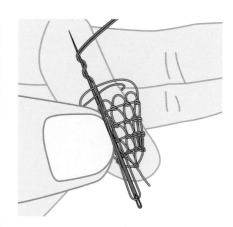

5 Wrap the needle end of your new thread twice around the needle, anti-clockwise, as you would when making a regular knot.

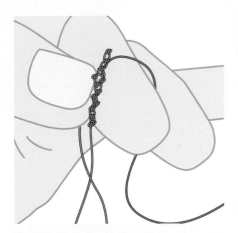

3 Now wrap the working end of the new thread across the top of your index finger and hold in place using your middle finger.

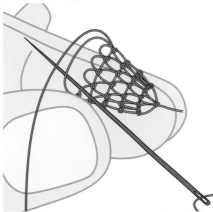

4 Pass the needle through the last loop you made, under the thread made by the reverse knot, and then under the new thread.

THE OLD THREAD

Leave the tail of the old thread lying to the left and do not take it in to your work. Once you have completed a row, you may cut the old thread's tail shorter if it is interfering with your work. If you believe the knot is secure enough, cut the thread close to the knot. However, it is preferable to leave a short tail of about 1cm (½in) and tuck it in later to the back of the work (see page 126).

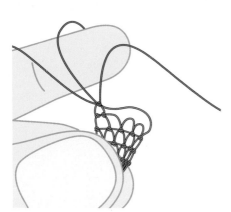

6 Tug at the knot you have made with extra firmness to secure the new thread into your work.

7 Continue to make a row of loops in the normal way, using your new working thread.

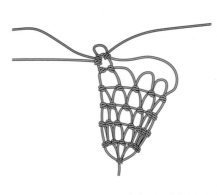

8 You will have achieved a simple integration of the new thread and can continue with the schematic.

Assembling a Flower

As you grow accustomed to making oya needle lace and gain more experience, you will soon discover your own way of working the techniques, especially the assembly of the different parts of each flower. There are several ways to do this and you will almost certainly find the easiest and most practical one for yourself. Having said that, there are two common methods for assembling the separate parts of a flower project.

Using a Tail Thread

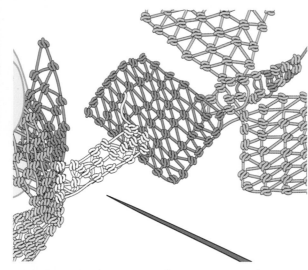

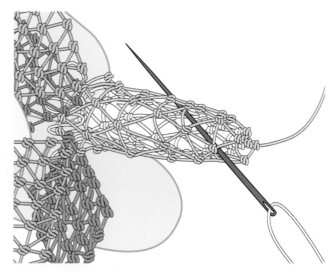

1 Having left a tail of about 10cm (4in) at the base of an inner stem, thread this on your needle. Insert the needle into the hollow centre of your outer stem and out through the tip at the bottom.

2 As the needle passes through the tip of the outer stem, it will pull the inner stem into place. Once the two (or more) pieces are positioned correctly, turn the needle and make a few small stitches around the stem to secure it all in place (see page 126).

Using a Separate Thread

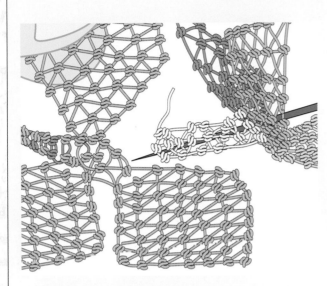

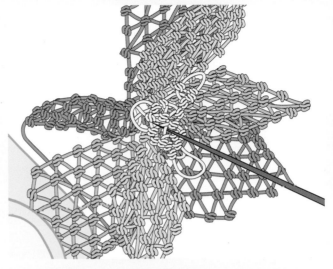

1 Thread your needle with a new length of thread – one of the colours used for the flower. A length of about 22cm (8½in) will do. Knot the end. Nudge the tip of the inner stem into the hollow centre of the outer stem. You can do this by hand or using the tip of your needle. Now pass the needle through the centre of the inner stem and into the hollow centre of the outer stem.

2 Keep going straight until the needle passes out through the very tip of the outer stem.

When assembling needle lace flowers with multiple petals (such as the Cheery Daffodil, pages 24–27, the Oriental Lily, pages 48–53 and the Festive Poinsettia, page 90–95), remember to arrange inner and outer stems so that the petals alternate in the round, rather then align with each other. This gives flowers a more realistic, three-dimensional appearance.

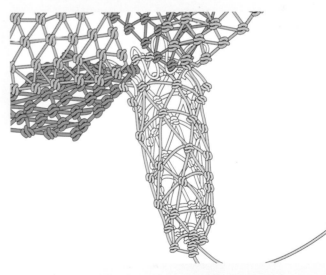

3 Turn the needle and make a couple of small stitches around the stem. When you are satisfied that the parts are securely connected, knot the thread and trim any loose ends.

Finishing

As you complete each stem, leaf or petal, there will be loose threads that need trimming and tucking in, and several pieces may need to be assembled in order to make a whole (see Assembling a Flower, pages 124 to 125). The techniques are very simple and, if you have tied your knots tightly, perfectly adequate.

Casting Off

Ensure your final knot is extremely secure and tight and cut the thread as close to the knot as possible.

Stitching

Using the same colour thread as your flower, make a number of very small running stitches.

Weaving in Ends

Tuck in straggly tails or threads using the tip of your needle. Just poke them anywhere in between the loops and threads at the under side of your work. Tuck in just enough of the tail (about 1cm/½in) so that it doesn't come away and then cut it off if the tail is really long.

SECURE KNOTS

If you are unsure of cutting so near to the knot, you can create your own method of securing the knot after cutting, such as leaving the tail long and weaving it in at the back of the piece. You should be able to find a method that is comfortable for you.

OYA TERMINOLOGY

Hoop The starting point of all oya, made when casting on and into which all base loops are made.

Loop Formed each time you make a knot. Each row or round of a piece is made from a given number of loops.

Needle threads The two threads at the eye of the needle, and which are wrapped around the stem of the needle each time a knot is made.

Picot A complex loop for a more frilly effect.

Reverse knot A knot made by drawing the working thread across the top of your work from right to left; enables you to build rows working from left to right.

Round Stems are made in rounds, rather than rows, forming a tube.

Row Flat pieces – stems and petals – are built in rows.

Schematic A diagram given for each part of the flower, which shows the number of rows or rounds a piece has and the number of loops in each one.

Simple base The foundation of a stem, leaf or petal; the basic number of loops onto which subsequent rows or rounds are built.

Tail thread When casting on, this is the thread to the left of the first knot made. It remains redundant and is trimmed close to the knot on completion of the work.

Working thread When making rounds or rows, the working thread is always to the immediate left or right of the last knot made.

Index

Acknowledgements

The flowers were designed and created with the help of two dear friends, both talented oya crafters: Nermin Buyukkorkmaz, who has been crafting with me and teaching me for many years; and Sibel Kucuk, who owns the gorgeous oya blog: sibelincicekleri.wordpress.com, where she creates free-form styles of oya as she sees them in nature.

Though historical records about oya barely exist, I have nonetheless found the encyclopedic publication *Oya Culture Since the Ottomans*, by Taciser Onuk, absolutely invaluable in my research.

I would also like to thank Marcia Young of US *Fiber Art Now* magazine for giving me the opportunity to write my first article about oya needle lace; the Golcuk Municipality Arts and Culture Center for introducing me to many talented craftswomen and giving me precious insight into how I could showcase their beautiful crafts on a global platform.

It would have been impossible for me to complete this book without the incredible patience, support and guidance of my editor, Anna Southgate, and I also thank Caroline Smith and my parents for believing in my ability when the project was first suggested. Thank you to my husband, Mustafa, for taking over all of the roles required, despite his busy job, to keep the house and children running smoothly while I concentrated wholly on cracking ahead with this book.

Flower Design

Sibel Kucuk: Purple Hyacinth; Cheery Daffodil; White Apple Blossom; Wild Violets; White Jasmine; Pretty Forget-me-nots; Frilly Dahlia; Calla Lily; Blooming Begonias; Winter Roses; Mexican Shellflower; Elegant Chrysanthemum.

Figen Cakir: Purple Hyacinth; Wild Violets; White Jasmine; Oriental Lily; Dainty Daisy; Pink Carnation; Frilly Dahlia; Winter Roses; Festive Poinsettia; Elegant Chrysanthemum.

The flowers were made by:

Nermin Buyukkorkmaz: Purple Hyacinth; Cheery Daffodil; White Apple Blossom; Wild Violets; Pretty Forget-me-nots; Oriental Lily; Dainty Daisy; Pink Carnation; Frilly Dahlia; Calla Lily; Blooming Begonias; Winter Roses; Mexican Shellflower; Festive Poinsettia; Elegant Chrysanthemum.

Sibel Kucuk: Cheery Daffodil; White Jasmine; Frilly Dahlia; Elegant Chrysanthemum.

Figen Cakir: Cheery Daffodil; Pink Carnation; Frilly Dahlia; Winter Roses.

Picture credits

Corbis Images: Mauricio Abreu, p 9; **Gap Photos:** pp 89, 90; **Hulton Archive:** pp 7, 11, 12; **Shutterstock:** Pavel Vakhrushev p 22, Muellek Josef p 26, Nataliia Melnychuk p 30, Olga Miltsova p 31, haraldmuc p 34, MarkMirror p 37, Snowbelle p 42, ekawatchaow p 43, Bo Valentino p 46, Steve Bower p 50, Julietphotography p 53, Jana Behr p 56, Daniel Prudek p 57, Suslik1983 p 62, Vilor p 66, KAppleyard p 67, memaggiesa p 70, Web Picture Blog p71, Madlen p 76, Wutthichai p 79, LanKS p 84, AdStock RF p 85, Elena Talberg p 88, Rose-Marie Henriksson p 92, oksana2010 p 95, Volosina p 98, **Owen Suen** p 101; **Victoria & Albert Museum:** pp 10, 14, 15; www.oldschoolhijabi.com: p 12; www.trekearth.com: p 8.